SEWING MACHINE

MACHINE

SECRETS

First published in the United States by

Interweave Press LLC
201 East Fourth Street
Loveland, CO 80537
www.interweave.com

Copyright © RotoVision 2012

ISBN: 978-1-59668-603-8

Library of Congress Cataloging-in-Publication Data not available at time of printing.

COMMISSIONING EDITOR: Isheeta Mustafi
PROJECT EDITOR: Cath Senker
ART DIRECTOR: Emily Portnoi
ART EDITOR: Jennifer Osborne
DESIGN: Clare Barber
COVER DESIGN: Adrian Newman
ILLUSTRATIONS: Rob Brandt
PHOTOGRAPHY: Sherry Heck
STYLIST: Heather Sansky

SEWING MACHINE
SECRETS

The insider's guide to mastering your machine

Nicole Vasbinder

INTERWEAVE
interweave.com

Contents

SECTION 1
CHOOSING MACHINES AND ACCESSORIES

SECTION 2
SEWING MACHINE FEET AND HOW TO USE THEM

How to use this book

I have been sewing for about 30 years and consider myself a fairly advanced seamstress. Most of my sewing is straightforward construction for clothing, handbags, and home décor projects; it primarily involves seams, hems, buttonholes, and zippers. I was hesitant to try embellishing techniques because I have basic sewing machines and thought I needed a fancy embroidery machine. Then I discovered that a wide variety of feet and attachments make impressive designer techniques possible and easy to do on any home sewing machine.

Knowing which machine is right for you is the first important step to learning how to sew. Knowing how to use that machine inside and out is crucial in order to make the most out of it. You can use your sewing machine for more common sewing tasks and also learn techniques that most people think only high-end machines can achieve. In this book, you will learn all about the feet and attachments that are available and how to use them for their intended purposes as well as for other tasks you may not have even imagined.

This book is organized into two sections. Section one is all about showing you how to choose, use, and maintain a sewing machine, and learning handy tips along the way so you can extend the life of your machine. I discuss all the different types of sewing machines and the tasks for which they are best suited. I cover mechanical and computerized machines and their advantages and limitations. I also explain how to clean, oil, and maintain your sewing machine so that it runs like new and stays out of the repair shop. I show you which parts are simple to replace as they wear out.

Section two is technique based and is organized into chapters according to individual sewing tasks such as zippers, hems, and embroidery. Each chapter identifies the most versatile and commonly used presser feet, and then provides step-by-step tutorials for all the results you can achieve with these feet. I explain how each foot can be used and manipulated to help you improve your sewing skills, providing useful tricks and insider secrets along the way. Tutorials are identified by skill level and include illustrations of how the finished item should look (see the tutorial icons key below).

Whether you are just starting out with your first sewing machine or have been sewing for a while and want to build on your skills, this book gives you practical advice and tips to help extend the life of your sewing machine and master a broad range of techniques. I sincerely hope that this book becomes an inspiring part of your sewing library and pushes you to a new level of creativity and confidence.

Happy sewing!

Tutorial icons

Beginner

Intermediate

Advanced

Finished item icon

Glossary

appliqué
A technique in which a piece of fabric is sewn on top of another piece of fabric. Also refers to ready-made appliqué patches.

backstitch
Reverse stitches at the beginning and end of a seam used to secure the threads and prevent the seam from coming undone.

basting
A temporary seam using very long stitches. Can also be used to gather fabric by pulling on the bobbin threads. Basting stitches are removed when they are no longer needed.

bias grain
The 45-degree angle on fabric between the length and cross grain. Fabrics stretch on the bias.

binding
A narrow strip of fabric cut on the bias or cross grain to give stretch, which is wrapped around an edge to finish it neatly. Used on necklines, armholes, and hems, and also on seam allowances.

cross grain
On a fabric weave, the threads that run from selvedge to selvedge. Also known as the weft.

couching
A technique of stitching down cords and yarns onto the surface of a fabric as a decorative embellishment.

edgestitch
Stitching very close to an edge or seam line. It is usually ⅛" (3 mm) or less.

facing
A piece of fabric sewn to an edge and turned to the inside to conceal seam allowances and finish edges.

feed dog
The teeth under the needle plate on a sewing machine that move the fabric.

grainline
Usually refers to the length grain on fabric, but also refers to the printed grainline on a pattern.

hem allowance
The total amount of fabric included on a pattern for a hem.

interfacing
A material used to stiffen, strengthen, or stabilize another fabric. Can be fused on or sewn in.

length grain
On a fabric weave, the threads that are parallel to the selvedge. Also known as the warp.

nap
The raised surface on a fabric such as velvet where all the fibers are pointing in one direction. Napped fabrics must be cut as a one-way layout.

overcast
A seam finishing stitch where the threads wrap over the raw edge.

pinking
A seam finishing technique using pinking shears, which make zigzag cuts on the edge to prevent fraying.

pivot
A technique to stitch corners where you lower the needle in the fabric, lift the presser foot, and turn the fabric around the needle.

presser foot

Holds down the fabric against the feed-dog unit so it can move under the needle. Some presser feet are basic and some are for specialty applications.

raw edge

The unfinished, cut edge of a piece of fabric.

right side

The side of fabric that will be visible from the outside of a finished project. Often abbreviated as RS.

satin stitch

Zigzag stitches that are very closely spaced. They are used as embroidery, for monograms, and for stitching on appliqués.

seam

A line of stitches that joins two pieces of fabric.

seam allowance

The distance between a seam and the raw edge. Most patterns have seam allowances included and they are usually ⅝" (16 mm).

seam finish

A technique to prevent the raw edge of a fabric from fraying and raveling. Common seam finishes are pinking, zigzag, binding, and serging.

selvedge

The finished edges down either side of a length of fabric. They are frequently printed with manufacturer's information and are more tightly woven than the rest of the fabric.

serge

The chain stitch produced by a serger or overlock machine. Can be used as a construction seam or seam finish.

shank

Attaches a presser foot to a sewing machine. Machines are designed for low shank, high shank, or slant shank. Some feet are attached to a shank and some snap on to a shank.

stay stitch

A line of stitches used to stabilize an edge and prevent it from stretching.

topstitch

Stitching close to an edge or seam line. It is usually ¼" (6 mm) from the edge.

warp

On a fabric weave, the threads that run parallel to the selvedge. Also known as the length grain.

weft

On a fabric weave, the threads that run from selvedge to selvedge. Also known as the cross grain.

wrong side

The side of fabric that will not be seen on the outside of a finished project. Often abbreviated as WS.

CHOOSING MACHINES AND ACCESSORIES

There are many different types of sewing machines available, from basic mechanical machines to top of the line computerized embroidery machines. Some features on a machine are essential, while other optional accessories are useful. If you take care of your machine, it will last forever.

Types of Machines

Sewing machines

All sewing machines have the same basic purpose: they make a lockstitch using an upper thread and a bobbin thread to connect two layers of fabric. All sewing machines have a feed dog that pulls fabric through the machine, a presser foot to hold the fabric against the feed dog, and a needle to go through the fabric to connect the threads.

General sewing machines

The sewing machine may have one basic straight stitch, several basic utility stitches, or many utility and decorative stitches. It will have settings to adjust the stitch length and may also have settings to adjust the type of stitch, stitch width, and needle position.

Sewing machines can be mechanical or computerized. Mechanical machines use gears, belts, and cams to change stitches and move the parts of the machine. Dials and levers adjust the settings. Computerized machines have buttons to control computer chips and circuits that adjust the settings.

Machines come with either a front-load (a) or a top-load (b) bobbin. Bobbin mechanisms are either a rotary hook or an oscillating hook. Rotary-hook bobbins, found on older machines and new high-end machines, spin in a continuous circle. They tend to be quiet and have few thread jams. Oscillating hooks, found on lower-priced machines, rotate back and forth. Both rotary and oscillating hooks are available on either top-load or front-load machines.

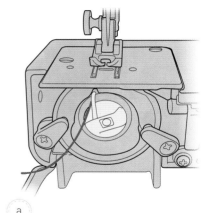

a

b

Embroidery machines

- Embroidery/sewing combo machines and embroidery-only machines are available

- Stitch elaborate designs at the touch of a button

- Work with an embroidery hoop to move the fabric

- You can buy designs on cards, disks, or from the Internet

Embroidery machines are computerized and can stitch elaborate designs at the touch of a button. Some are embroidery and sewing combo machines while others are embroidery-only machines. If you already have a sewing machine that you love, consider purchasing an embroidery-only machine because this will be less costly than a combo.

Like sewing machines, embroidery machines use a needle thread and a bobbin thread to form a lock stitch. They work with an embroidery hoop that attaches to the machine bed. The hoop then moves the fabric as the needle stitches out the design. Embroidery machines have digital displays to adjust the settings and some have large touchscreen capabilities. Using the powerful editing capabilities, you can enlarge, rotate, and mirror image a design. The memory function allows you to save and combine different designs. Embroidery machines come installed with many designs; additional designs can be added using insertable cards or disks. Most also have a USB port so that you can link up a computer to the machine and download designs from the Internet.

 INSIDER SECRETS

You can stitch many basic embroidery stitches and monograms on a general sewing machine using special feet—see Chapter 14 for all of these feet:

Satin stitch foot
Appliqué foot
Open-toe foot
Patchwork foot
Free-motion embroidery foot
Flower attachment
Circle attachment

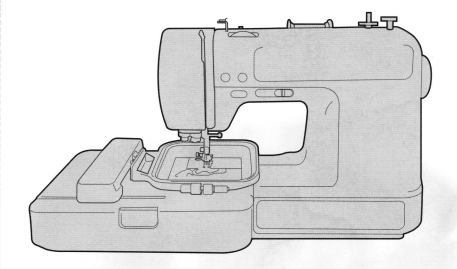

Serger/overlock machines

- Uses loopers instead of bobbins
- Creates a chain stitch that can stretch
- Can have two-, three-, four-, and five-thread capabilities
- Used to stitch and finish a seam in one operation
- Can be mechanical or computerized

a

INSIDER SECRETS

Sergers cannot be used to install zippers and or stitch buttonholes, so they complement a general sewing machine. You can mimic many of the functions of a serger on a general sewing machine.

Sergers are also known as overlockers or overlock machines **(b)**. They make a chain stitch, cut and neaten the fabric, and stitch and finish the seam allowance in a single operation **(a)**. They can be used for seaming, hemming, and edging. Sergers are also extremely useful for sewing knits because a chain stitch can stretch. Sergers operate much faster than general sewing machines and can create very professional results.

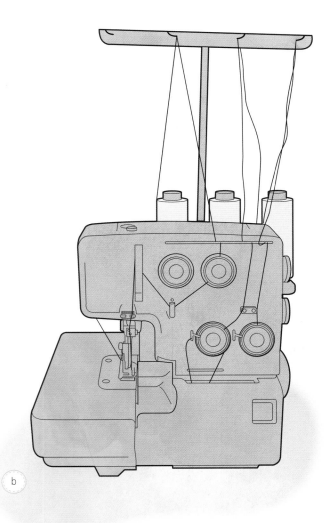

b

Coverstitch machines

- Uses loopers instead of bobbins

- Creates a two- or three-stitch cover hem

- Creates a two-thread chain stitch

- High-end five-thread sergers can often convert to cover-hem capabilities.

- Should have a free-arm function for sleeves and trouser legs

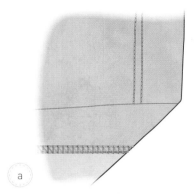

a

INSIDER SECRETS

You can stitch a faux coverstitch on a general sewing machine using a twin needle. The bobbin thread will zigzag back and forth between the two needles and will be able to stretch.

A coverstitch machine **(b)** creates a cover hem that looks like two rows of straight stitching on the right side and a chain stitch on the reverse side **(a)**. Some advanced coverstitch machines can also do a three-stitch cover hem that uses three needles and a looper. Most machines can stitch a two-thread chain stitch that can be used for seaming. High-end coverstitch machines have adjustable needle positioning so that you can sew cover hems with the needles closely spaced or farther apart. Many of the top-quality five-thread sergers can convert to coverstitch capabilities.

Like a serger, a coverstitch machine does not use bobbins and has settings to adjust the length of the stitches. It has a differential feed to create gathers. The coverstitch machine does not have knives. Instead, the fabric moves flat through the machine. Many machines have optional binder accessories, so you can stitch bound necklines on T-shirts using a cover hem. They have a free-arm function so you can easily hem sleeves and trousers.

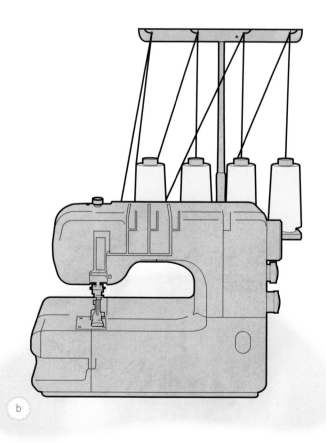

b

2

Sewing Machine Buyer's Guide

Anatomy of a sewing machine

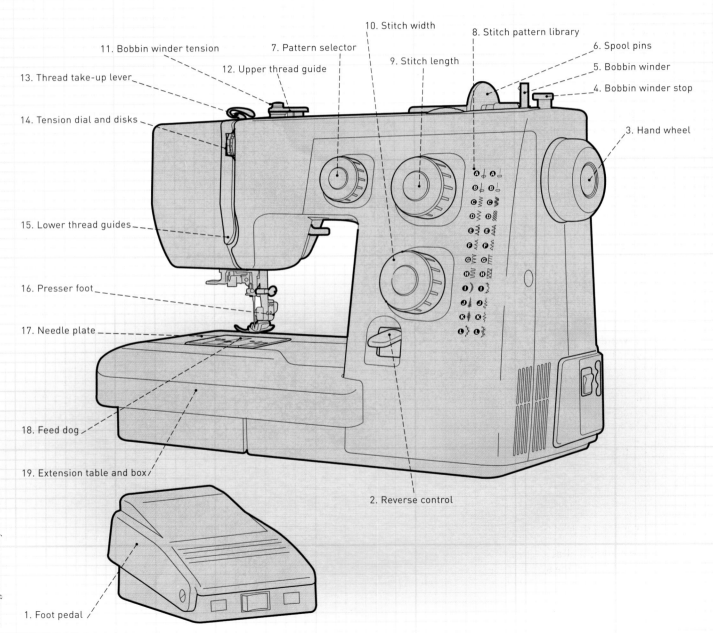

10. Stitch width

8. Stitch pattern library

11. Bobbin winder tension

7. Pattern selector

9. Stitch length

6. Spool pins

12. Upper thread guide

5. Bobbin winder

13. Thread take-up lever

4. Bobbin winder stop

14. Tension dial and disks

3. Hand wheel

15. Lower thread guides

16. Presser foot

17. Needle plate

18. Feed dog

19. Extension table and box

2. Reverse control

1. Foot pedal

1. Foot pedal
Press down on the foot pedal to operate the machine. Some computerized machines have a power button that bypasses the foot pedal to operate the machine automatically.

2. Reverse control
This makes the feed dog turn in the opposite direction and moves the fabric toward you as you sew. It is used to lock in the stitches.

3. Hand wheel
Also known as the fly wheel or balance wheel, it can be used to operate the machine by hand but it also turns when the foot pedal is pressed. Computerized machines automatically disengage the hand wheel when winding bobbins, but on most mechanical machines it is disengaged manually.

4. Bobbin winder stop
This stops the bobbin from winding when the bobbin is full.

5. Bobbin winder
This holds the bobbin in place for thread to be wound onto it.

6. Spool pins
These hold the thread on the sewing machine. Spool pins can be vertical or horizontal. Many machines have two so that two threads can be used at the same time with a twin needle.

7. Pattern selector dial
This is turned to select the symbol of the required stitch pattern. On computerized machines, stitches are selected on a menu screen.

8. Stitch pattern library
This diagram shows all the stitches that the machine can make. Some machines make just a few, while very high-end machines can make hundreds.

9. Stitch length
This controls the speed of the feed dog in relation to the needle. The longer the stitch, the faster the feed dog pulls the fabric through, and the farther apart the stitches are. Most modern machines measure from 0 to $\frac{1}{16}$" (0 to 4 mm); some higher-end machines go up to $\frac{1}{4}$" (6 mm).

10. Stitch width
This controls how far the needle can swing to the left or right from the center. Most machines can make a $\frac{1}{16}$"- (4 mm) wide stitch but some can go up to $\frac{1}{3}$" (9 mm) wide. Adjusting the stitch width can also change the needle position to the left or right for straight stitching if the machine does not have a separate needle-position adjuster.

11. Bobbin winder tension
The thread passes between these small round disks to keep an even tension on the thread when winding a bobbin.

12. Upper thread guide
The thread passes through this after leaving the spool pin and before passing through the tension disks.

13. Thread take-up lever
The thread passes though the small eye at the front after going through the tension disks. It moves up and down with the needle and should be in the highest position at the beginning and end of a seam to prevent threads from tangling.

14. Tension dial and disks
These are two metal disks that are side by side; the thread goes between the disks. The tension disks control the speed of the top thread. The dial usually goes from 0–9: 0 is the loosest tension and 9 the tightest. It is normally set to 4. Looser tension spreads the disks apart and creates more room for the thread to pass through faster, while tighter tension brings the disks closer together and slows the thread down.

15. Lower thread guides
All machines have a guide right above the needle to help the thread go straight down into the fabric with the needle. Some machines have additional bonus guides above the needle guide.

16. Presser foot
Holds the fabric against the feed dogs.

17. Needle plate
Also called the face plate or throat plate, the needle plate has a hole for the needle to pass through and also has markings for seam guides. For top-load bobbins, there is a separate plate that slides forward for access.

18. Feed dog
This moves in an elliptical motion; the little teeth grip the bottom layer of fabric and move the fabric upward as the needle makes the stitch.

19. Extension table and box
These can be removed for free-arm sewing when sewing narrow tubes such as trouser hems and sleeves. They should also be removed to allow access to the front-load bobbins.

Quality of construction

A major factor in the cost of a sewing machine is the quality of its construction. A high-quality machine will last forever if it is well maintained with regular cleaning.

A good machine should have the following features:

- The machine is made of mostly metal parts and strong plastics. Weak plastics can crack over time.

- The machine is quiet, even at high speeds.

- The machine has a multi-part feed-dog unit, which will give a good grip on the fabric and pull it through evenly.

- The hand wheel should turn smoothly without slipping or jamming.

- The foot pedal is sensitive and responsive. It should not slide around.

- The presser-foot pressure works just as well on the thinnest silks as it does on the thickest wools and denim. Some machines have a pressure regulator while some are automated with a spring.

- A good hook stops the threads from jamming in the bobbin at the beginning of a seam.

- A well-designed threading path and tension disks prevent the threads from becoming unthreaded or tangling in the upper threading.

- The weight of the machine prevents it from traveling on the table as you sew, even at high speeds.

- The timing is perfect between the needle thread and the bobbin threads. This helps to eliminate skipped stitches.

 INSIDER SECRETS

You can obtain a quality machine at any price point. Just because a machine is more expensive does not necessarily mean that it is better. Vintage machines may not have all the features of a new machine, but many are well made, retain their resale value, and are very collectible.

Motor power and speed

Another major factor in determining the price of a machine is its motor. A good machine has a powerful motor that can sew through many layers of fabric. A weak motor will sew well on two layers of quilting cotton, but may struggle on thick materials such as upholstery fabrics.

You should always test out a machine before you purchase it. Sewing-machine dealers usually have demonstration machines on the selling floor for you to try out. Sewing-machine dealers always use thin cottons as test fabrics on which to demonstrate machines because all machines sew well on these fabrics, so when you test out machines, bring your own fabrics. Try sewing on nine layers of denim—you will have to sew across that many layers at the inside ankle when hemming jeans.

Another feature to check before purchasing is the speed of the machine: some are very fast and some are very slow. If you are sewing many long straight seams, a high-speed motor speeds up the task.

Most general machines can achieve 600 stitches per minute. Some machines marketed to quilters and professional sewists can sew very fast with speeds of 1,600 stitches per minute.

INSIDER SECRETS

Some machines have a setting to adjust the speed. This is useful if you tend to be heavy footed and sew too quickly. Simply slide the speed control to a slower speed. No matter how firmly you press the foot pedal, the machine will not be able to go faster than that setting.

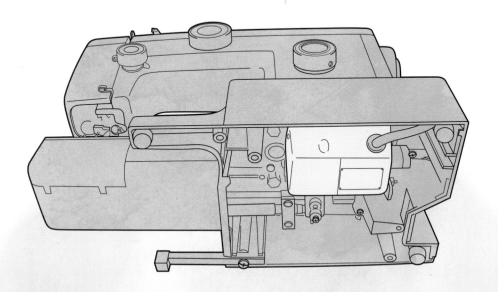

Common accessories and feet

Some sewing machines come equipped with many accessories and feet while other machines do not.

If you buy a machine with few accessories and feet, you may spend more money in the long run than if you had bought a machine that included them in the selling price. If the desired feet and accessories are not included, check if they are readily available. Find out if you can use generic feet or only brand specific feet. Generic feet tend to be lower-priced.

 INSIDER SECRETS

Machines also typically come with a screwdriver, seam ripper, a package of replacement needles, and three to four extra bobbins.

Feet and accessories typically included with most machines	Feet and accessories typically included with high-end machines	Feet and accessories typically sold separately
Zigzag/all-purpose foot	Zigzag/all-purpose foot	Invisible zipper foot
Zipper foot	Straight stitch foot	Shirring/gathering foot
Buttonhole foot	Satin stitch foot	Ruffler attachment
Button foot	Zipper foot	Felling foot
Rolled hem foot	Buttonhole foot	Side-cutter attachment
Blind hem foot	Button foot	Open-toe foot
Overedge/overcast foot	Rolled hem foot	Appliqué foot
	Blind hem foot	Teflon foot
	Overedge/overcast foot	Roller foot
	Walking/even-feed foot	Knit/tricot foot
	Quilting bar	Cording foot
	Binding foot	Pintuck foot
	Free-motion embroidery foot	Piping and welting foot
	Quarter-inch foot	Sequin and ribbon foot
		Beading foot
		Fringe foot
		Stitch-in-the-ditch foot
		Flower attachment
		Circular attachment

Common stitches

Some sewing machines have a large number of utility and embroidery stitches while others may have just a few basic stitches. Many stitches are purely decorative and you may not use them often. Here are the essential stitches you will use most often.

Straight stitch (a)
This is the main construction stitch that is used for 99 percent of sewing. It is used for seams, topstitching, mending, and hems. Straight stitch does not stretch, so it is not suitable for stretch knits.

Zigzag (b)
The zigzag stitch can be used as a decorative topstitch, to finish seam allowances to prevent fabric edges from fraying, as a satin stitch to sew on appliqués and stitch monograms, for sewing stretch knits, and for sewing on buttons.

Buttonhole (c)
A buttonhole is a box made of tiny zigzag stitches. It is possible to stitch a buttonhole using the zigzag stitch, but it is much easier and faster to use a buttonhole stitch. Mechanical machines do a four-step buttonhole, while computerized machines do an automatic or one-step buttonhole. Some machines offer different types of buttonholes, such as keyhole buttonholes and special buttonholes for knits.

Tricot/elastic stitch (d)
This stitch is known as the three-step zigzag. It is used to attach elastic and stitch on knit fabrics. The stitches are smaller than a standard zigzag, so there is less chance the stitches will snag, but the stitch has lots of stretch.

Stretch straight (e)
This stitch makes one stitch forward, one back, and one forward. It is very durable because it goes over the same spot three times, and it is often used for high-stress seams. It can also be used for knits; the stitch has built-in stretch because the feed dog stretches the fabric slightly.

Overcasting (f)
The overcast stitch uses both zigzag and straight stitches. It is used to finish the raw edges of fabric to prevent fraying.

Blind hem (g)
The blind hem makes several tiny zigzags and then one large zigzag. It is used for hemming and is practically invisible from the right side.

Decorative embroidery
Many machines offer a variety of decorative stitches, such as satin stitches, flowers and leaves, cross-stitch patterns, and more.

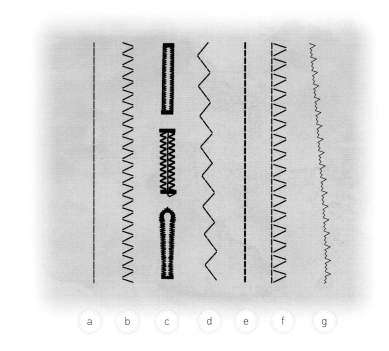

a   b   c   d   e   f   g

Sewing machine features

Most machines offer a variety of features to automate tasks and facilitate sewing. Many of these features used to be available only on high-end sewing machines, but some are now standard on new models.

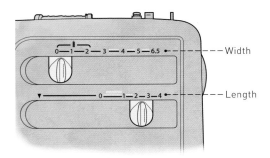

Stitch length and width (essential)

A good machine should have the capability to adjust both the length and width of the stitches. Most machines have a maximum width and length of 4 mm, while more advanced machines offer widths up to 9 mm and lengths up to 7 mm. Many computerized machines automatically adjust the length and width for each stitch but these default settings can be adjusted.

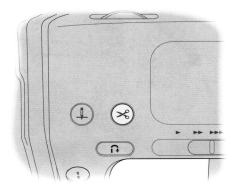

Thread cutter (optional)

Sewing machines have a manual razor cutter on the left side of the machine, while vintage machines have a manual cutter on the back of the needle shaft just above the needle. Many computerized and embroidery machines have an auto-thread cutter that cuts the thread tails at the push of a button.

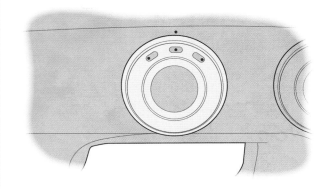

Adjustable needle position (essential)

Needle in the center position is the default. It is common to be able to adjust the needle left of center for zippers and piping. Many machines also offer a needle right option, which is useful for edgestitching.

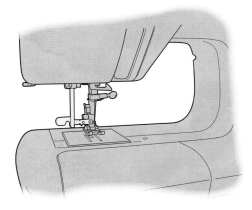

Threading aids (optional)

Because threading the needle can be difficult, many machines offer a needle threader. It is a little hook that catches the thread and pulls it through the needle. Some advanced sergers have jet-air threading, where you simply drop the thread into a hole, push a button, and a jet of air pushes the thread through the threading path.

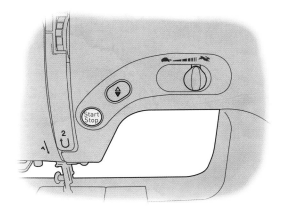

Start/stop (optional)

With computerized and embroidery machines you can bypass the foot pedal; you can sew by simply pushing the start button. This is handy when sewing long seams and embroidery because it can reduce body strain from continuous pressing on the foot pedal.

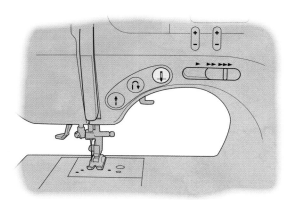

Needle up/needle down (optional)

This sets the needle to always end in the down position and is a time-saver when doing pivot turns and embroidery. It can be set to end in the up position for seaming and piecing.

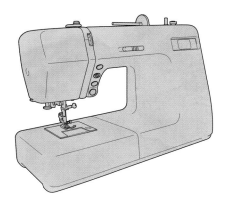

Lock/fix-stitch (optional)

Rather than backstitching at the beginning and end of a seam, you can do a fix-stitch, which is made up of several stitches right on top of each other. They are practically invisible and are used for decorative stitches, embroidery, and quilting. Lock/fix-stitch is offered on most computerized machines.

3

Mechanical Versus Computerized

Mechanical machines

Mechanical and computerized sewing machines each have characteristics that make them wonderful and they also each have some drawbacks. Being aware of the positives and negatives of each type will help you choose a machine that is right for you.

Pros

Basic
Mechanical machines tend to be simple to operate and have few options. They are excellent for beginners and children.

Affordable
These machines are often much less expensive than a comparable computerized machine that has similar stitches. They are perfect as a secondary machine to take to classes or as a backup if your main machine is in the repair shop.

Easy to maintain
Because mechanical machines do not have computer components and circuits, it is simple to clean and fix them at home. If you clean and oil a mechanical machine regularly, you might never have to take it into a repair shop to be serviced. If a mechanical machine does need to be repaired at a shop, it is often a simple job with a quick turnaround and low cost.

Sturdy
Most mechanical machines are hardy. Older models in particular tend to be formed mostly of metal casings and beds. They are well made and can withstand a few bumps and scrapes without the risk of damage to the interior components.

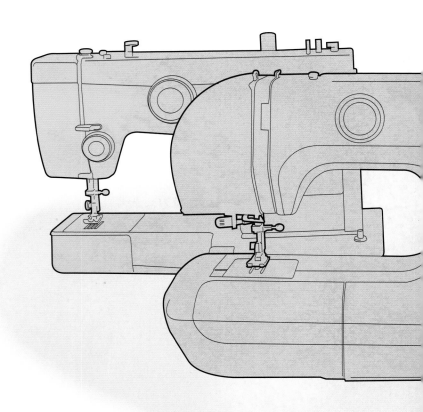

Cons

Heavy
Mechanical machines can be extremely heavy; some "portable" vintage machines that can weigh upward of 30 pounds (14 kilos). However, lightweight models are available. If you will need to move the machine frequently, make sure you can lift it easily.

No automatic buttonhole
Most mechanical machines do not have a one-step buttonhole function, which can make it difficult to create identical buttonholes on a garment that has many buttons. Mechanical machines cannot do specialized buttonholes.

Fewer stitches
Mechanical sewing machines do not have nearly the number of stitches that even a basic computerized machine offers.

Manual settings
It is necessary to manually adjust the length and width when changing stitches on a mechanical machine. Sometimes this requires using trial and error, which can be time consuming.

Fewer options
Most mechanical machines do not have bonus features such as a lock/fix-stitch option, needle up/needle down, or a start/stop option.

Limited customization
Most basic mechanical machines have a maximum stitch length of 4 mm and a maximum stitch width of 4 mm, while computerized machines can do longer and wider stitches to provide more stitch options. They may have a needle left and right, but it is not incremental.

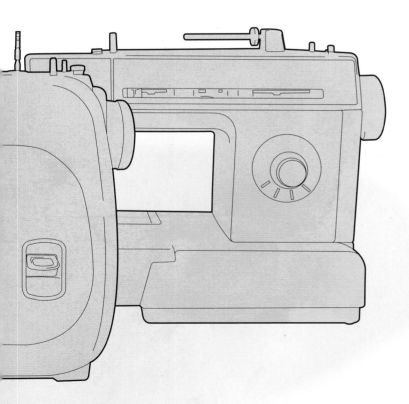

Computerized machines

Pros

Quiet
Computerized machines tend to be very quiet even at high speeds. This is helpful, especially for sewing late at night.

User friendly
Computerized machines are very easy to operate because most functions are automated. When a stitch is selected the machine automatically adjusts to a default length, width, and needle position. Most advanced machines have a sewing advisor on the display that advises the correct presser foot to use and shows a picture of the stitch.

More stitches
There are many more decorative and utility stitches offered on computerized than on mechanical machines. Many come equipped with alphabet fonts that can make monograms simplicity itself.

Embroidery
Even a basic computerized machine offers some simple embroidery stitches, while the fancier sewing/embroidery machines do elaborate embroidery patterns. High-end embroidery machines can digitize a drawing and stitch it out at the touch of a button.

Memory
Most computerized machines have a memory function so that stitch combinations can be saved to use again.

Buttonholes
All computerized machines offer a one-step buttonhole and most have other types of buttonholes such as those for knit fabrics or keyhole buttonholes.

Bonus functions
Features such as needle up/needle down, start/stop, and lock/fix-stitch are standard on even the most basic computerized machines. These machines also have a speed control feature.

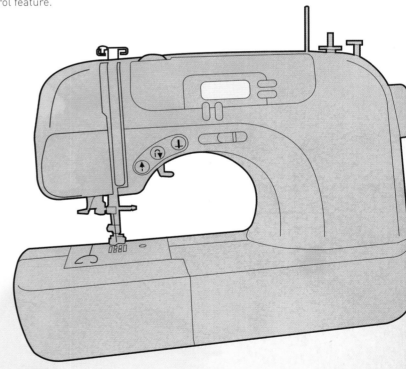

Cons

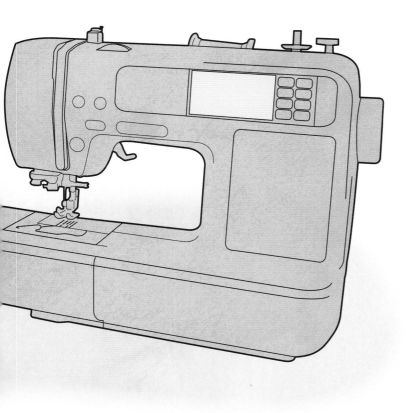

Price
This is the biggest downside to computerized machines; they are nearly always more expensive than similar mechanical machines. Beware of a bargain-basement computerized machine because it may have problems.

Repairs
Computerized machines can be hard to fix yourself because they have circuit boards and computer chips that may need repair. If the machine does need to be repaired, note that many sewing-machine repair shops send out computerized machines to the factory, and the turnaround time can be much longer than for a mechanical machine repair. If you do not have a backup, you might be without a machine for weeks.

Delicate
Many computerized machines, particularly lower-quality models, are made of lightweight plastics. Thin parts, such as spool pins and needle threaders, can break off easily.

4

Sewing Machine Needles

Anatomy of a needle

All needles designed for general sewing machines work with any brand and model of machine and are labeled as system 130/705 H or 15x1 H. There are many different types of machine needles, each designed for different threads, fabrics, and tasks. Machine needles have different sized eyes, different points, and different scarves.

Parts of a needle

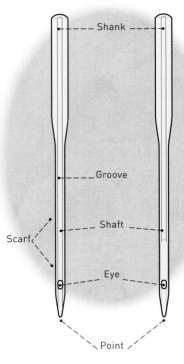

FRONT   BACK

Shank
Groove
Shaft
Scarf
Eye
Point

Shank
Needles made for general sewing machines have a flat back on the shank.

Blade/shaft
The needle size is the measurement of the diameter of the blade. As the needle gets wider, the eye gets wider.

Groove
The front of the needle has a long groove that cradles the thread as it penetrates the fabric.

Scarf
This is the indentation above the eye on the back of the needle. It helps the bobbin hook to catch the needle thread. Some needle types have specially shaped scarves.

Eye
This is the hole that the needle thread passes through.

Point
The needle point is designed to penetrate the fabric without damaging it. Some needle types have sharp points and others have blunt points.

INSIDER SECRETS

- Always keep a supply of spare needles on hand in case of breakages.

- Universal needles are the most common type of needle and are available in every size. Other types, such as stretch and metallic, come in a limited range of sizes.

- Do not throw away old needles in the garbage. They could cause injury. Place bent pins and old broken needles in a small plastic container, such as a used yogurt cup. When the container is full, tape it shut, label it, and throw it away.

Needle sizes

Needles always have two numbers to indicate the size. The first number is the European size and it measures the diameter of the needle blade. The second number is the American size and this number is arbitrary.

A size 80/12 needle measures 0.8 mm in diameter. Smaller numbers mean thinner needles, while larger numbers mean thicker needles. Sewists generally prefer the needle to make the smallest hole possible to avoid damaging the fabric.

SEWING-MACHINE NEEDLE SIZES		
American		European
Lightest	8	60
	9	65
	10	70
	11	75
	12	80
	14	90
	16	100
	18	110
Heaviest	19	120

How to change a needle

Needles need to be changed if the needle breaks, becomes worn out or dull, or a different type or size needle is required. It is quick and easy to do this.

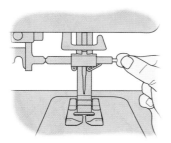

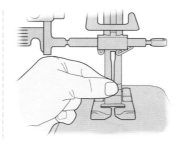

1 Remove the old needle by turning the screw above the needle clamp toward you a half turn. Slide the needle down and out of the shaft.

2 Make sure the flat side of the new needle is toward the back, insert it into the shaft until it cannot go up any more, and tighten the screw using a screwdriver.

In general, it is wise to insert a new needle every three or four projects, or eight hours of sewing time. Every time the needle makes a stitch, it penetrates multiple layers of fabric and dulls a little. A dull needle causes skipped stitches, can damage the fabric, is prone to breaking, and can cause thread jams. Change needles even more frequently when sewing delicate fabrics.

TOOLS

- Screwdriver
- Fresh needle

Types of needles

Universal needle

- Has a slightly rounded point
- A multipurpose needle for most sewing tasks
- Use with all-purpose cotton or polyester thread
- Designed for most fabric types
- Available in the full range of sizes

A universal needle is an all-purpose needle that can be used for most sewing needs. It features a slightly rounded point and can be used for seams, buttonholes, decorative stitches, and sewing on trims. Use it with all-purpose cotton or polyester thread. You can use it for many fabric types and it should be your default needle. Universal needles come in all sizes from 60/8 up to a 120/19; size 80/12 is the most commonly used. Use finer needles on delicate fabrics and heavier needles on thicker fabrics.

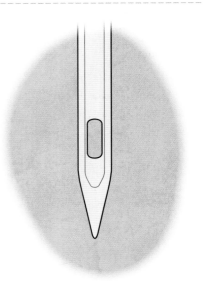

Microtex needle

AT A GLANCE

- Has a very fine, sharp point
- Used for seams, decorative stitching, and topstitching
- Use with all-purpose cotton or silk thread
- Designed for thin and delicate fabrics
- Use with a straight stitch foot and needle plate for straight seams.
- Available in sizes 60/8, 70/10, 80/12, 90/14, 100/16, and 110/18

Microtex needles feature a very fine, sharp point designed to easily pierce through thin and delicate fabrics. Use Microtex needles when sewing lightweight fabrics such as silk chiffon and organza, cotton lawn, microfiber, polyester silkies, and lamé. Use them for perfectly straight topstitching. They are ideal for piecing together quilt tops and for other tasks where precision is paramount. For perfectly straight seams, use with a straight stitch foot and a straight-stitch needle plate. Use Microtex needles with all-purpose cotton or silk thread. They are available in sizes 60/8, 70/10, 80/12, 90/14, 100/16, and 110/18.

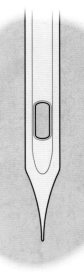

Denim/jeans needle

- Has a sharp point and extra-strong blade

- Used for seams and topstitching

- Use with all-purpose thread

- Designed for thick and heavyweight fabrics

- Use with a roller foot for uneven thicknesses

- Available in sizes 70/10, 80/12, 90/14, 100/16, and 110/18

Denim needles feature a sharp point and a very strong blade. Use them when sewing heavyweight or tightly woven fabrics such as denim, canvas, and upholstery fabrics. These needles are designed to pierce through thick fabrics easily without breaking and are perfect for hemming jeans. A denim needle is ideal paired with a roller foot to sew over thick and uneven layers. Use denim needles with all-purpose cotton or polyester thread. They are available in sizes 70/10, 80/12, 90/14, 100/16, and 110/18.

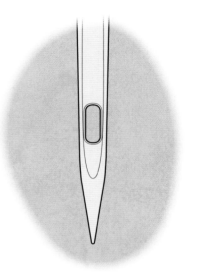

INSIDER SECRETS

- Needles come in packages with assorted sizes or all one size. You may like to buy one assorted pack and a pack featuring the size you use most, for example, the 80/12.

- A needle will always follow the path of least resistance. If there is an opening in the weave of the fabric slightly left or right of the seam, the needle will slide down there. Normally, this is not noticeable in seams that will be pressed open, but it can be an issue in topstitching. Microtex or denim needles are more accurate.

Ballpoint/jersey needle

- Has a rounded point
- Used for seams and hems
- Use with all-purpose polyester thread
- Designed for knit fabrics
- Use with a knit foot or even-feed foot to prevent fabric from rippling
- Available in sizes 70/10, 80/12, 90/14, and 100/16

Ballpoint needles feature a rounded point and are designed to slide between fibers rather than cutting through them. Use these needles when sewing knit fabrics to avoid causing runs and damage to the fabrics. They are perfect for jersey, interlock, and sweater knits. Use ballpoint needles with all-purpose polyester thread. They are available in sizes 70/10, 80/12, 90/14, and 100/16.

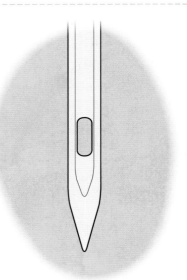

 INSIDER SECRETS

Always do a test stitch when sewing knits, trying both a ballpoint and stretch needle. Check for skipped stitches and damage to the fabric, then use the needle that performs best.

Stretch needle

- Has a slightly rounded point and a deep scarf
- Used for seams and hems
- Use with all-purpose polyester thread
- Designed for stretch knits that have spandex
- Use with a knit foot or even-feed foot to prevent the fabric from rippling
- Available in sizes 75/11 and 90/14

Stretch needles feature a slightly rounded point and a deep scarf. Like ballpoint needles, they are designed to slide between fibers rather than cutting through them. However, the deep scarf helps the needle thread to catch the bobbin hook better than a ballpoint needle, which prevents skipped stitches. Use stretch needles when sewing stretchy knit fabrics that have spandex, such as swimsuit fabrics or jersey and interlocks with spandex. If the fabric is stretching, pair this needle with a knit foot or an even-feed foot. Use stretch needles with all-purpose polyester thread. They are available in sizes 75/11 and 90/14.

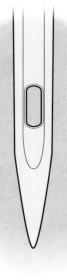

Leather needle

- Has a wedge cutting point
- Used for seams and hems
- Use with all-purpose polyester thread
- Designed for nonwoven materials such as leather and vinyl
- Use with a Teflon foot or an even-feed foot
- Available in sizes 70/10, 80/12, 90/14, 100/16, and 110/18

Leather needles feature a sharp wedge-shaped point rather than a tapered point. This special tip is designed to cut cleanly through leather and suede without causing damage. Leather needles are also ideal for other nonwoven materials such as plastic, vinyl, and oilcloth. Pair with a Teflon foot or an even-feed foot. Use with all-purpose polyester thread and lengthen the stitch to 3 mm. Leather needles are available in sizes 70/10, 80/12, 90/14, 100/16, and 110/18.

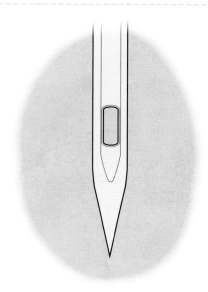

 INSIDER SECRETS

Never use a leather needle on knits or wovens because the cutting point will cut a large hole in the fabric that causes tearing.

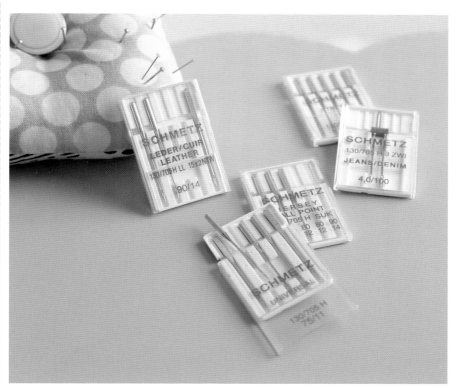

Embroidery needle

- Has an enlarged eye and wide groove
- Used for decorative stitches and embroidery
- Use with rayon and other types of embroidery thread
- Use with a satin-stitch foot, free-motion embroidery foot, and other decorative feet
- Available in sizes 75/11 and 90/14

Embroidery needles feature a slightly rounded point, an enlarged eye, and wide groove. The eye and groove accommodate thick embroidery threads. The deep scarf helps to prevent skipped stitches. Pair an embroidery needle with any foot for decorative stitching, such as a satin-stitch foot, free-motion embroidery foot, or circular sewing attachment. Use embroidery needles with rayon or other embroidery threads. They are available in sizes 75/11 and 90/14.

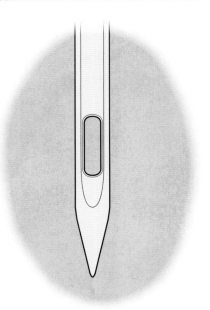

Quilting needle

- Has a sharp point and a tapered blade
- Used for machine quilting
- Use with all-purpose cotton thread
- Use with an even-feed/walking foot or free-motion embroidery foot
- Available in sizes 75/11, 80/12, and 90/14

Quilting needles feature a sharp point and a tapered blade. The blade is designed to easily penetrate multiple layers of lofty fabric without damaging the materials when machine quilting. The sharp point ensures very straight stitches. Pair a quilting needle with an even-feed/walking foot and a quilting bar for rows of quilting stitches or with a free-motion embroidery foot and an embroidery hoop. Use quilting needles with all-purpose cotton thread. They are available in sizes 75/11, 80/12, and 90/14.

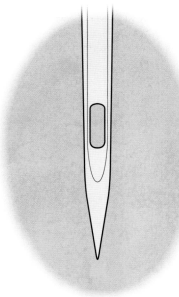

Metallic needle

- Has an elongated coated eye
- Used for decorative stitching
- Use with decorative metallic and other novelty threads
- Use with a satin-stitch foot or other decorative feet
- Available in sizes 80/12 and 90/14

Metallic needles feature a slightly rounded point and an elongated coated eye. The special eye is designed to protect delicate metallic and novelty threads and prevent them from shredding when sewing decorative stitches. Pair a metallic foot with any foot for decorative stitching such as a satin-stitch foot, free-motion embroidery foot, flower attachment, or circular sewing attachment. Use metallic needles with any metallic decorative thread. They are available in sizes 80/12 and 90/14.

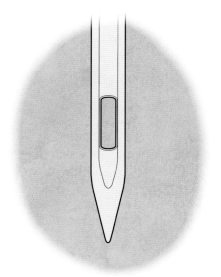

 INSIDER SECRETS

Sew slowly when working with metallic threads. Some of these threads will fray at high speeds even when using a metallic needle.

Twin needle

- Has two needles attached to one shank
- Used for decorative stitching, pintucks, and faux coverstitch hems
- Available in various sizes and spacing
- Available with universal, stretch, jeans/denim, metallic, and embroidery needles
- Use appropriate thread for the needle type
- Try with a satin-stitch foot, pintuck foot, or even-feed/walking foot

Twin needles feature two needles attached to one shank. Use these for decorative stitching, pintucks, topstitching, or faux coverstitch hems. You can buy a twin needle that has stretch needles, denim/jeans needles, metallic needles, embroidery needles, or universal needles. Twin needles can be spaced closely together or farther apart, and this distance is the first number on the size. The second number is the size of the needles. For example, a 4.0/100 twin denim/jeans needle features denim needles that are a 100/16 size and are 4 mm apart. Use twin needles with a standard needle plate because you need space in the needle hole to accommodate two needles. Pair them with feet for decorative stitches such as a satin stitch foot or a flower attachment. Use twin needles with a knit foot or even/feed foot to hem T-shirts. Use them with a pintuck foot for perfect pintucks. Twin needles come in a variety of sizes and spacing for universal needles: 1.6/70, 1.6/80, 2.0/80, 2.5/803.0/90, 4.0/804.0/90, 4.0/100, 6.0/100, and 8.0/100. They are available in limited sizes for other select needle types: Stretch 2.5/75 and 4.0/75, Jean/Denim 4.0/100, Metallic 2.5/80 and 3.0/90, and Embroidery 2.0/75 and 3.0/75.

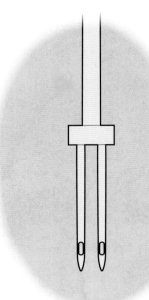

Triple needle

- Has three needles attached to one shank

- Used for decorative stitching, topstitching, and hems

- Available only with universal needles

- Available in sizes 2.5/80 and 3.0/80

- Use with all-purpose cotton, polyester thread, or silk thread

 INSIDER SECRETS

Try using a slightly different color thread in each needle for a beautiful ombré effect.

Triple needles feature three needles attached to one shank. Use these for decorative stitching, topstitching, and fancy hems. Triple needles are available only with universal needles in a limited range of sizes and spacing. The spacing is measured between the two outside needles. Make sure you are using a standard needle plate. Use the triple needle with all-purpose threads or silk thread. Triple needles come in sizes 2.5/80 and 3.0/80.

Topstitch needle

- Has an elongated eye

- Used for topstitching

- Use with topstitching and other heavy threads

- Use with a straight-stitch foot and needle plate

- Available in sizes 80/12, 90/14, and 100/16

Topstitch needles feature a sharp point and an elongated eye and a sharp point. The large eye is designed to accommodate thick topstitching thread. The sharp point will help to give perfectly straight topstitching and penetrate through many layers of fabric. Use topstitch needles with thick topstitch thread or buttonhole thread and pair with a straight-stitch foot and straight-stitch needle plate. These needles are available in sizes 80/12, 90/14, and 100/16.

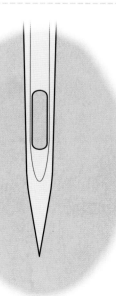

5

Threads

All-purpose threads

All-purpose cotton and polyester threads are used for nearly all sewing tasks from basics seams to buttonholes and machine embroidery.

Cotton thread

AT A GLANCE

- Used for basic seams as well as buttonholes and decorative stitches

- Use a universal, Microtex, or quilting needle sized for the fabric

- Excellent for delicate fabrics such as silk chiffon, cotton voile, and lawn

- Has no stretch and should not be used for knits

- Stitches can be pressed flat into the fabric to hide the stitches on lightweight and delicate fabrics

Cotton all-purpose sewing thread can be used for both machine and handsewing. Because cotton is a natural fiber, stitches sewn with cotton thread can be ironed and the stitches will flatten out and disappear into the fabric. This is great for lightweight fabrics such as silk chiffon and cotton voile, because you cannot see the bumps from the stitches. However, cotton thread is not as strong as polyester and is more susceptible to deterioration from exposure to sunlight, detergents, perspiration, and age. This is not a major problem when using delicate fabrics because the items tend not to be exposed to heavy wear and tear. Cotton threads have little elasticity and should not be used to sew knits as the stitches will be prone to breaking.

INSIDER SECRETS

- Never use cotton thread when sewing leather. The tannins in the leather will destroy it. Always use polyester thread when working on leather projects.

- Never use old thread, as it deteriorates with age and becomes weak and brittle. Do not use thread on wooden spools; thread has not been produced on wooden spools since the 1980s.

Polyester thread

- Much stronger than cotton thread and will not shrink

- Has elasticity and is ideal for stretch knits

- Good for a variety of fabrics including quilting cottons, denim, wool, and leather

- Used for basic seams as well as buttonholes and decorative stitches

- Use a needle designed and sized for your fabric

INSIDER SECRETS

When matching a thread color, unwind a single strand of thread from the spool and lay it on your fabric. Squint your eyes and choose a color that disappears. If you are deciding between two colors, always select the darker color; it will disappear into the fabric while lighter colors tend to show.

Polyester all-purpose thread can be used for machine and handsewing. Much stronger than cotton, it is ideal for projects that will be subjected to heavy use such as jeans, jackets, and pillows. It resists shrinking and is colorfast. Polyester thread has a bit of stretch and is perfect for stretch-knit fabrics; it should be used with a ballpoint or stretch needle. Because polyester thread is made from synthetic material, the thread will always stay round and you cannot press the stitches flat. Keep this in mind if you are working on very thin fabrics, because the stitches could show. Also, polyester thread can be stronger than some delicate fabrics such as cotton voile and when stress is put on a seam, the fabric is more likely to tear than the stitches.

Specialty threads

Specialty threads are used for embellishments, handsewing, and special-purpose sewing.

Silk thread

- Used for hand basting and machine embroidery
- Used for sewing silks and other fine fabrics
- Tighten the tension slightly

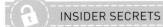 INSIDER SECRETS

In the most common sizing system for thread sizes, the higher the number, the thinner and finer the thread. All-purpose thread is usually a size 50.

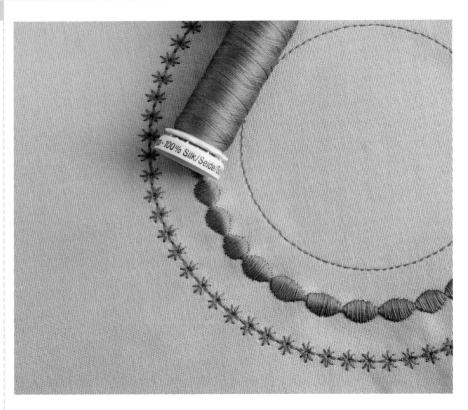

Silk thread is thinner than all-purpose cotton and polyester threads and is very lustrous. You can stitch seams with it, and it is ideal for sewing on silk and other fine fabrics. When machine stitching with silk thread, use a fine needle such as a Microtex needle and tighten the tension slightly. You can also use silk for machine embroidery, although bear in mind that you will need a large quantity of thread, which can prove costly. Silk is perfect for hand basting since the smooth nature of silk thread allows temporary stitches to be easily removed.

Elastic thread

- A stretchy thread used for elastic shirring
- Only used in the bobbin
- Hand wind onto the bobbin
- Available in black and white

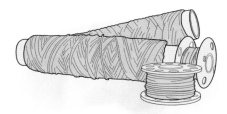

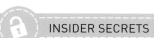 INSIDER SECRETS

To create more gathers, steam the completed rows to shrink the elastic thread.

Elastic thread is a very stretchy thread made with a rubber core and is used for elastic shirring. It is used only in the bobbin and must be hand wound onto it. It generally comes in black and white; in the upper thread, use an all-purpose thread in the color of your choice. As you stitch multiple rows of elastic shirring, the fabric gathers up. This technique is frequently used to gather waists and cuffs.

Invisible thread

- Used when you do not want to see stitches on hems or embellishments
- Comes in clear or smoke colors
- Made of nylon or polyester

 INSIDER SECRETS

Lower the temperature on your iron when pressing on top of nylon stitching because nylon has a low melting point.

Invisible thread is very thin and made of either nylon or polyester. It comes in clear for light-colored fabrics and smoke for dark colors. It works well for blind hems and for sewing on trims and appliqués and can be used in the loopers on a serger for decorative effects. Brands of invisible thread vary in thickness, so it may be necessary to adjust the tension. Use all-purpose thread in the bobbin because you may not be able to wind invisible thread on a bobbin.

Topstitch thread

- Used for topstitching seams on heavy-duty fabrics
- Use with a topstitch needle
- Also used for handstitching on buttons

 INSIDER SECRETS

Topstitch thread comes in a limited range of colors but you can mimic the look of it by using two strands of all-purpose thread through the eye of a topstitch needle.

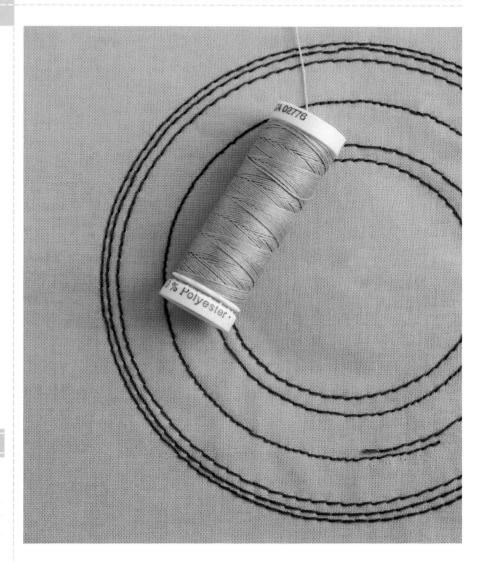

Topstitch thread is a strong thread made of polyester and is thicker than all-purpose thread. It is often used in a contrasting color on jeans. You will need to lower the upper tension to accommodate the thicker thread and use all-purpose thread in the bobbin. A topstitch needle is required when using this thread because it has a large eye. Topstitch thread is also an excellent choice for handstitching on buttons.

Upholstery thread

- Mildew, chemical, and UV resistant

- Used for upholstery, slipcovers, handbags, and leather projects

- Use a heavy needle and a long stitch length

 INSIDER SECRETS

If using upholstery thread to machine stitch leather, use an appropriately sized leather needle and a walking foot or Teflon foot.

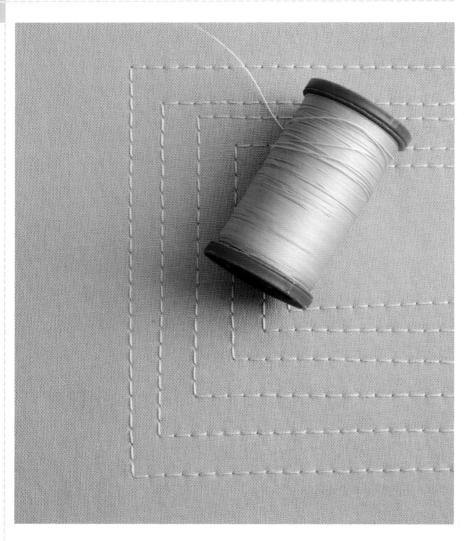

Upholstery thread is a heavyweight thread made of nylon and is exceedingly strong. It is mildew, chemical, and UV resistant and is used for upholstering furniture and sewing slipcovers. Upholstery thread can be used for both indoor and outdoor applications. It can be used for sewing leather and is a good choice for sewing handbags. Use a 100/16 or 110/18 denim needle with upholstery thread and 3 mm stitch length. It comes in a limited range of colors.

Embroidery thread

- Shiny and smooth thread used for machine embroidery
- Use with an embroidery needle
- Used only in the upper threading

 INSIDER SECRETS

Bobbin-fill thread is a very thin thread used to fill bobbins for machine embroidery. Embroidery uses large quantities of thread and you can fit more thread on a bobbin if it is thinner. It comes in black and white and you can purchase pre-filled bobbins.

Embroidery thread, either 100 percent rayon or viscose, is used for machine embroidery. It is very shiny, smooth, and lustrous. Embroidery thread was initially developed as a more affordable alternative to silk. It comes in a wide variety of both solid and variegated colors. It should be used only in the upper threads while all-purpose thread or bobbin-fill thread is used in the bobbin. You can also try using embroidery thread in the loopers on a serger. Use an embroidery needle and check the tension because it may need to be tightened.

Metallic thread

- Used for decorative stitches and embroidery

- Always use a metallic needle to prevent fraying and breaking threads

- Can also use metallic threads in the loopers on a serger

If you are experiencing frequent thread breakages, sew slowly to eliminate some of the stress on the thread.

Metallic thread can be used for machine embroidery, monograms, decorative stitching, and topstitching. You can also use metallic thread in the loopers on sergers for decorative serged edges. It has a polyester or nylon core, which is wrapped in metallic fibers and films. It can also be made of rayon. Metallic thread can kink, fray, and break with universal needles so you should always use a metallic needle.

Quilting thread

- Used exclusively for hand quilting
- Specially coated to prevent tangling
- Do not use on a sewing machine

 INSIDER SECRETS

Never use hand-quilting thread in your machine because the special coating can rub off on the tension disks and gum up your machine.

Hand-quilting thread, made from 100 percent cotton, is used for handstitching on quilts and for other handstitching. It has a special glazed coating to give added strength and smoothness and prevent tangling. This thread is not a good choice for machine stitching because it is stiff and does not move through the machine well or wind onto a bobbin. It comes in a limited range of colors.

6

Attachments

Useful attachments

Various attachments can make your sewing easier, faster, and more fun.

Needle plate

- Zigzag needle plates have a wide needle hole
- Straight-stitch needle plates have a small, round needle hole

The needle plate, also known as the face plate or throat plate, has an opening for the feed dog and a hole for the needle to pass through. Standard needle plates have a wide hole to allow for zigzag stitching **(a)**, but you can also obtain a straight stitch needle plate that has a small, round needle hole **(b)**. The straight stitch plate, used with a straight stitch foot, produces perfectly straight stitches. The small hole supports the fabric and prevents the needle from pushing the fabric down into the hole. Sometimes the needle plate can get gouges around the needle hole. This is caused by the needle hitting the edges of the hole. If the plate is damaged, replace it to prevent thread from catching and shredding.

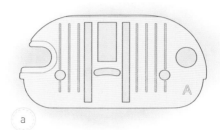

a

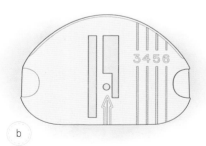

b

 INSIDER SECRETS

An alternative to a straight-stitch plate is to put adhesive tape over the sides of the wide hole on a standard zigzag plate. The tape will support the fabric. Clean off any sticky adhesive residue before you use the plate for zigzag stitching again.

Adjustable seam guide

- Magnetic seam guides attach to the needle plate at the desired seam width

- Can cause problems on computerized sewing machines

- Screw-in seam guides screw in to the machine bed and have an adjustable bar

- Sold at any fabric store; screw-in types are sold by machine dealers

INSIDER SECRETS

You can use blue painters' tape from the hardware store as a seam guide. Tape it on the needle plate at the correct seam width. It is low-priced, easy to see, and does not leave a sticky residue.

Although the needle plate has seam guide markings on it, these can be difficult to see. You can attach an adjustable seam guide to the needle plate or machine bed to provide a clearer guide. A magnetic seam guide is a chunky metal block with a strong magnet on the bottom that attaches to the needle plate at the seam measurement you require **(a)**. Magnets can be detrimental to computers, so avoid using them on computerized sewing machines. They are sold at any fabric store.

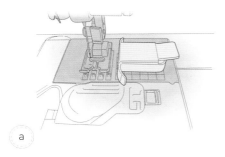

You can also obtain a seam guide that screws into the threaded screw hole on the machine bed to the right of the needle plate **(b)**. It has a bar that can slide to the desired position. This type of seam guide is often included with higher-end sewing machines; it can also be purchased from a sewing-machine dealer or online.

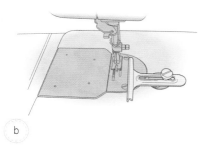

A quilting bar is attached into a slot on the back of a walking foot and is used for quilting evenly spaced lines **(c)**. You determine the width of the space by adjusting the quilting bar. You can also insert the bar into some shanks.

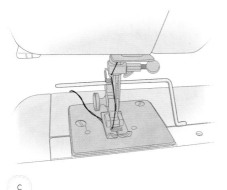

Extension table

- Creates an extended sewing surface for large projects
- Comes in various sizes
- Attaches to the free arm on the machine

Extra-large extension tables attach to the sewing bed to give you a much larger flat sewing surface. They are very useful when you are working on big projects such as quilts or curtains because they support the weight of the fabric. Extension tables come in various sizes; some of the most popular are 10" × 17" (25 × 43 cm) and 18" × 24" (46 × 61 cm). Many have measurements along the front to use as a quick measuring tool. Extension tables are simple to install. Just remove the flat bed on the machine to expose the free arm and snap in the extension table. Sewing machines marketed to quilters often come with an extension table, but they are also available from sewing-machine dealers or online. Some machines are not able to take an extension table, so double-check before purchasing one.

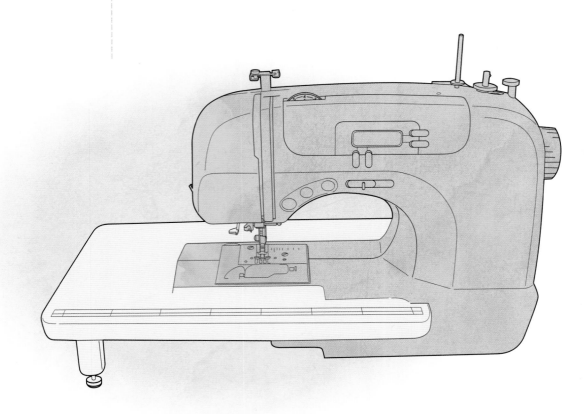

Knee lift

- A removable rod at the front of the machine that raises the presser foot
- Only included on high-end machines

INSIDER SECRETS

You can remove the knee lift when it is not needed or you have to transport the machine.

Some sewing machines have a knee-lift feature, which is an extended rod on the front right of the machine. You push the rod to the right with your knee to lift the presser foot, which allows you to keep both hands on the fabric. This is a huge time saver when you are stitching items that have many pivot turns, such as pockets and pillows, or when doing appliqué. You can still use the presser foot lever at the back of the machine if you prefer because the knee lift does not override the lever. It is only offered on high-end machines and cannot be added onto machines.

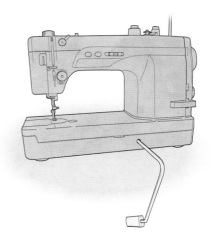

Darning plate

AT A GLANCE

- Simulates a lowered feed dog
- Included with machines that have no feed-dog drop
- Used when doing free-motion embroidery and monograms

INSIDER SECRETS

The darning plate can also be used when sewing on buttons instead of setting the stitch length to 0 mm.

A darning plate is a piece of plastic that snaps onto the needle plate to cover the feed dog and is used on sewing machines that do not have a feed-dog drop feature. It prevents the feed dog from having contact with the fabric and allows you to move the fabric. You use the darning plate for free-motion embroidery or monograms, or when using a flower attachment.

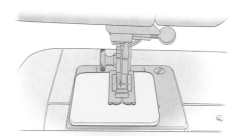

Embroidery hoop

- Standard embroidery hoops can be used on sewing machines

- Can be wood or plastic, square, or round

- Used for free-motion embroidery and monograms

- Use a hoop that is the appropriate size for the design

- Available at any craft store

While embroidery machines come equipped with embroidery hoops, general sewing machines do not. However, you can use a standard embroidery hoop normally used for hand embroidery on a general sewing machine to do free-motion embroidery, monograms, and more. Embroidery hoops are available in wood, metal, and plastic, and in various sizes. You can purchase round hoops and square hoops at any craft or fabric store.

You should use a size that is large enough for the design, but small enough to fit on the machine bed. To hoop the fabric, separate the rings and lay the fabric over the larger ring. Insert the smaller ring and tighten the screw.

 INSIDER SECRETS

Make sure that the fabric is stretched evenly and tightly in the hoop to prevent it from puckering during stitching. The movement of the needle can shift the fabric if it is not held firmly in the hoop. If you are using a lightweight fabric, you should also use a stabilizer.

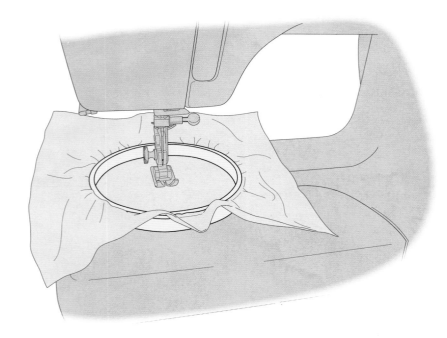

Dust cover

- Made of plastic, vinyl, or fabric
- Protects the machine from dust, dirt, and lint
- Has an opening for the handle so you can carry the machine with the cover

INSIDER SECRETS

Plastic covers are not breathable and can trap moisture underneath, which can damage the machine. You could sew a fabric cover or simply put a pillowcase over the machine.

A dust cover is a soft covering to protect the sewing machine from dust, dirt, and lint when not in use. Dust covers are generally made from vinyl or plastic. They have an opening for the machine's carrying handle so that you can carry the machine with the cover. The cover should be sized appropriately for the machine. Most sewing machines come with a dust cover, but they are often very thin and tear easily.

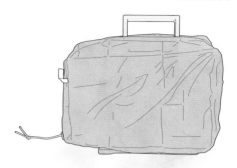

Hard case

AT A GLANCE

- Made of hard plastic to protect a machine from dirt and damage
- Two-part cases have a tray and lid that latch shut

INSIDER SECRETS

If you frequently transport your machine, consider buying a wheeled case. It has storage for the machine and supplies.

Hard cases are used to store and transport a sewing machine safely. They protect a machine from dust, dirt, and damage. Most hard cases have two parts: a tray and a lid that connect with hinged metal locks. The case is made from hard, strong but lightweight plastic and may have a built-in handle. Some cases are simply a hard plastic cover that slips over the machine and has an opening for the carrying handle. Vintage machines often have a hard cover that latches onto the machine itself. In the past, most sewing machines came with a hard case, but these days very few machines do. You can purchase a universal one from sewing-machine dealer or online.

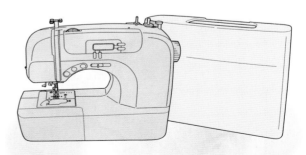

7

Sewing Machine Maintenance

Replacement parts

If the machine is used regularly, certain parts will wear out and will eventually need to be replaced. A sewing-machine repair shop can replace parts for you, but it can be straightforward and more economical to do it yourself.

Light bulb

AT A GLANCE

- Can be screw-in or push-in
- Always check the manual for the correct bulb for the machine
- Sold at fabric stores

All sewing machines have a light bulb above the needle area and sewing bed. Over time, the bulbs become dim and eventually burn out. Good lighting is essential when sewing; replacement light bulbs are sold at all fabric stores. Check the manual for any instructions about the type of bulb the machine uses. Some sewing machines use bulbs that screw in while others use bulbs that push and twist in. Open the left side of the machine above the needle to access the bulb.

INSIDER SECRETS

Keep several spare bulbs on hand and check the condition of the bulb every time you clean and oil the sewing machine.

Feed dog

- The feed-dog teeth can wear down with use
- Order online or from a sewing-machine repair shop
- Do not wind bobbins with the feed dog grinding against the presser foot

The feed dog is responsible for pulling the fabric under the presser foot. Eventually, the little teeth on it can become worn down and they can no longer grip the fabric firmly. When this happens, the fabric tends not to feed smoothly or it will drift as you are sewing. To replace the feed dog, remove the needle plate, unscrew the feed-dog unit, and replace with a new one. The feed dog is a part that is made specifically for each model of sewing machine, so make sure that the replacement is correct for your machine (using an incorrect feed dog could damage the machine). Order one on the Internet or from a sewing-machine repair shop.

 INSIDER SECRETS

Always disengage the needle and feed dog on the machine when you are winding a bobbin to prevent the feed dog from grinding against the bottom of the presser foot without a layer of fabric in between. Otherwise, the teeth will very quickly grind down to nubs.

Belt

- Can dry out and crack with age
- Come in different types and lengths for different models of machines
- Available on the Internet or at sewing-machine repair shops
- Universal stretch belts are sold at chain fabric stores

A sewing-machine belt is a ring usually made of rubber **(a)** that makes the hand wheel turn and makes all the parts of the machine move **(b)**. If the belt is old it can dry out and crack or stretch out. If this happens, then the sewing machine will not work. If you smell burning rubber, this is a sign that it is time to change the belt. Belts come in different lengths and can be smooth, notched, cogged, or cleated. It is important to purchase one that is the correct size and type for the sewing machine. You can order belts on the Internet or from a sewing-machine repair shop. It is also possible to buy a universal belt that will stretch to fit from any fabric store. Although universal belts are not ideal because they can stretch out quickly, they provide a useful standby. Open the right side of the machine to access the belt.

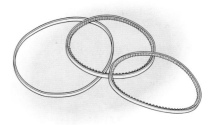

a

INSIDER SECRETS

Always make sure the machine is unplugged when replacing a belt.

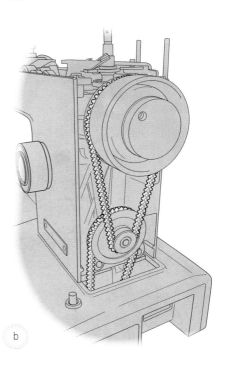

b

Bobbin

- Class 15 is the most common bobbin type
- Class 66 bobbins fit older Singer drop-in models
- Can be metal or plastic
- Singer Featherweight, Futura, and Touch and Sew models each have a specific bobbin

INSIDER SECRETS

Always check that the bobbin is not cracked, rusted, or bent. Roll it on a table and if it wobbles, throw it away.

While most machines come with three to four bobbins, it is sensible to purchase some additional ones to ensure that you always have an empty one ready to wind. Bobbins come in different sizes and shapes for different machines. The most common type is called a class 15 and it fits most front machines, while class 66 bobbins tend to fit older Singer drop-in models. Both types come in metal or plastic. There are bobbins designed exclusively for Singer Featherweight, Touch and Sew, and Futura machines. Some Elnas, Pfaffs, and Vikings have exclusive bobbins. Check the manual to see which type of bobbin your machine requires. You can purchase extra bobbins at any fabric store.

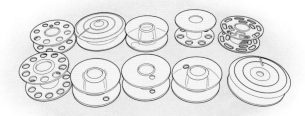

Bobbin case

- Adjust tension on a secondary bobbin case for specialty techniques
- Purchase bobbin cases from a sewing-machine dealer or online
- Use one designed for your machine

INSIDER SECRETS

To test the bobbin tension, remove the case from the machine, load a bobbin, and thread the case as usual. Hold by the thread tail and let the case dangle. The case should not slide when still, but should slide when you bounce the tail.

Having a second bobbin case on hand is wise because you can keep one with the tension normal for regular sewing and adjust the tension on the second one as needed for free-motion embroidery, elastic thread, or other techniques. To adjust the tension, simply turn the tiny screw to the left to loosen or to the right to tighten. You can do this on both removable and drop-in bobbin cases. You can purchase one from a sewing-machine dealer or online. Make sure to buy one that is made for your machine and model because many sewing machines use a specific type.

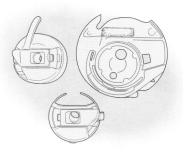

Cleaning the machine

Whenever you sew, the thread sheds fibers as it moves through the machine and leaves lint behind. As the needle punctures the fabric, this also leaves lint in the bobbin mechanism. If you do not clean the machine, the lint will mix with machine oil and create a nasty sludge that becomes caught in the gears of the machine and eventually stops the parts from moving. Cleaning and maintaining the sewing machine is the best way to prevent sewing problems and extend the life of the machine.

TOOLS

- Dusting brush
- Cotton swabs
- Cotton rag
- Rubbing alcohol
- Screwdriver

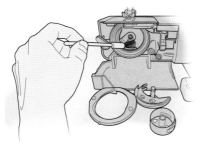

1 Unplug the machine and remove the needle, presser foot, and shank. Take out the bobbin case and bobbin hook assembly.

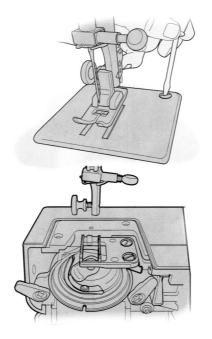

2 Take out the screws on the needle plate and remove the needle plate. Put all the removed parts in a cup to keep them together.

3 Use the brush to clean out the lint and dust from around the feed dog, through the threading path, and around the bobbin area.

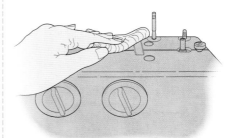

4 Dip the rag in rubbing alcohol and wipe the machine shell and bed to remove dust and lint.

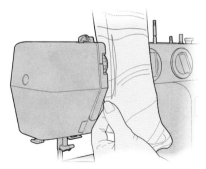

5 Dip the rag in rubbing alcohol and gently swipe it between the tension disks to remove lint and grime.

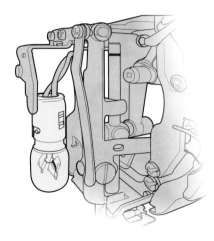

6 Open the left side of the machine to access the light bulb. It will either swing out or you remove a screw. Remove and clean the bulb. If it is burned out or dim, replace it.

7 Dip cotton swabs in rubbing alcohol and clean the bobbin case, bobbin hook, needle bar, and any other small places that you cannot reach with the rag.

IMPORTANT DON'TS

- Do not blow into the machine to remove dust because breath is damp and will introduce moisture into the machine that can cause parts to corrode.

- Avoid using cans of compressed air for cleaning because they also introduce moisture and push the lint farther into the machine. Instead, vacuum out the lint.

- Do not use sharp metal tools to pick out dust or you risk gouging metal parts that may then damage the thread.

INSIDER SECRETS

Rubbing alcohol works well to remove dirt and grease because it dries quickly and does not cause rust.

Oiling the machine

It is important to oil the machine to keep the metal parts moving freely. Check the manual for instructions as many machines have oiling holes. Some machines are sealed and self-lubricating and should never be oiled or you risk damaging the machine. Never oil plastic or nylon parts or gears. Once the machine is cleaned and oiled, it should run smoother and quieter.

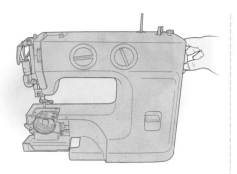

1 Turn the hand wheel toward you and look to see where metal parts move against each other. Stop when the takeup lever is in its highest position.

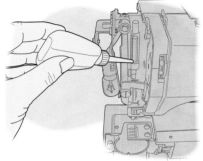

2 Put a drop of oil on the needle bar where it goes down into the shaft. Turn the hand wheel and you will see the bar stretch the oil up. When the bar is down, the oil will pool on the shaft.

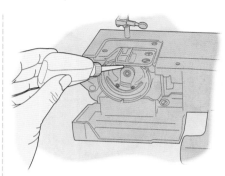

3 Put a drop of oil on the bobbin assembly and turn the hand wheel to distribute the oil.

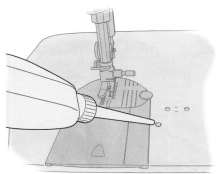

4 Put a drop of oil in all oiling holes (if the machine has them) and wipe off any excess with the rag.

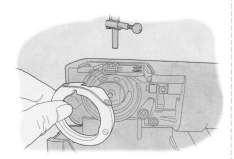

5 Reattach the presser foot and shank and insert a fresh needle in the machine. Reassemble the bobbin hook and race and close up the front and side of the machine.

6 Thread the machine and stitch over some scrap fabric to distribute the oil and to absorb any excess so that it does not damage a project.

Usually when people think their machine is broken, there is a simple solution. Here are the most common problems:

- The machine is incorrectly threaded on the top.
- The bobbin is in backward.
- The bobbin thread was not threaded through the bobbin case.
- The wrong type of bobbin is being used.
- The bobbin has been incorrectly wound.
- The needle is in backward or not pushed up all the way.
- The needle is worn out or bent.
- The machine is dirty and the threads are catching on lint.
- The machine needs to be oiled.
- The thread is of a poor quality.
- If the problem persists after checking all of these things, take the machine into the shop to be serviced.

INSIDER SECRETS

Use good-quality machine oil. You can purchase a bottle in the notions section of any fabric store. Avoid using baby oil or cooking oil.

SEWING MACHINE FEET AND HOW TO USE THEM

There are many different types of feet for the sewing machine. Some are more common and may come with the machine, while others are highly specialized and need to be purchased separately. The correct foot makes sewing easier and look much more professional. This section covers all the different types of sewing machine feet, what they are for, and how to use them.

8

Basic Feet

Types of basic feet

The basic feet are used for all day-to-day sewing. The classic zigzag foot can cope with virtually all sewing tasks, such as seams, embroidery, hems, seam finishes, and more. The straight stitch foot is used for seams and topstitching.

Zigzag foot

AT A GLANCE

- A general-purpose presser foot for most sewing tasks
- Used with all different weights of fabric
- Match the needle size and type to the fabric and thread
- Can be used with any thread types

INSIDER SECRETS

Most sewing machines can do a zigzag stitch with a maximum width of 4 mm. Some machines can do a wider stitch of up to 9 mm and therefore will use a zigzag foot with a wider slot. Do not use a zigzag foot with a narrower slot or the needle will break.

The zigzag foot (also known as the all-purpose foot) comes installed on most sewing machines. It can be made of metal or plastic and can be snap-on (a) or attached to a shank that screws onto the machine (b). It has a wide slot to allow the needle to swing back and forth without hitting the edges of the foot. Some zigzag feet have a small leveling button on the side to facilitate sewing over bumpy seams (c). It is designed for stitches that have width, such as zigzag or decorative embroidery (d). It is also necessary when using a twin needle or when adjusting the needle position right or left of center. There is a slight groove on the bottom that allows for the buildup of stitches when doing satin stitch or other dense decorative stitching. The zigzag foot is also used for basic straight stitching and for seams, topstitching, and hems.

Straight-stitch foot

- Used exclusively for straight stitches
- Helpful with seams on lightweight fabrics
- Used for perfect topstitching
- Match your needle size and type to your fabric and thread
- Usually used with all-purpose thread or topstitch thread

a

The straight-stitch foot has a small hole and is used for straight stitching with the needle in the center position (a). Some straight-stitch feet also have a left needle hole to allow for straight stitching with the needle in the left position. The tiny hole is designed to support the fabric and prevent the needle from pushing lightweight fabrics such as chiffon down into the needle hole. The bottom of the foot is very smooth to allow maximum contact with the feed dog for even stitches. The straight-stitch foot helps you to achieve accurate topstitching (b). For even more precise stitching, use a straight-stitch needle plate designed for the machine. Some straight-stitch feet have seam guides indicated on the toes to help with topstitching. The straight-stitch foot may come with higher-end machines, but often needs to be purchased separately.

b

INSIDER SECRETS

Some sewing machine feet come attached to a shank while other feet snap onto a shank that stays on the machine. If the machine is designed for screw-on feet only, you can purchase a snap-foot shank so that you can use feet that come only in the snap-on option. Sewing machines are designed to use either low-shank, high-shank, or slant-shank feet. Most home machines are low shank; vintage Singer machines tend to be slant shank, and high shank tends to be industrial machines. It is important to use the correct type for the machine.

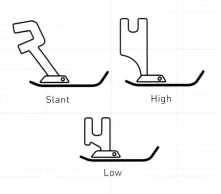

Slant   High

Low

Using basic feet

✿◌◌ Basic straight and curved seams

The basic seam is the building block on which all sewing projects are built. The secret to accurate and consistent seam allowances is to always keep your eyes and fabric edges on the seam guide. Never watch the needle because this can cause the fabric to drift.

TOOLS

- Zigzag foot or straight-stitch foot
- Adjustable seam guide (optional)
- Pins

1 Place the fabrics together with right sides facing and the raw edges aligned. Pin the layers together with the pins perpendicular to the seam line and ensure the pinheads are off the edge for easy removal.

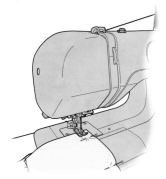

2 Place the fabric under the presser foot ¼" (6 mm) from the end. Line up the edges on the correct seam guide and lower the presser foot.

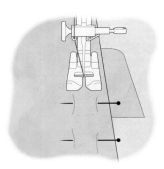

3 Backstitch to the end 5 or 6 stitches and then stitch forward, removing pins just before you stitch over them. Backstitch 5 or 6 stitches at the end, remove the fabric, and trim the thread tails.

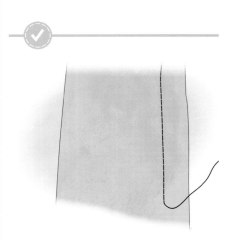

Pivot turns for corners and angles

TOOLS

- Zigzag foot or straight-stitch foot
- Adjustable seam guide (optional)
- Pins

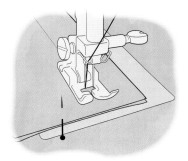

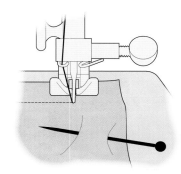

1 Stitch until you get to ⅝" (1.5 cm)—or whatever seam allowance you are using—away from the end. Stop and turn the hand wheel toward you to sink the needle in the fabric. If the machine has a needle down function, use that to sink the needle.

2 Lower the presser foot back down and keep stitching. There is no need to backstitch because you are working on the same seam, but in a new direction.

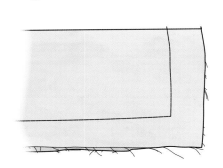

INSIDER SECRETS

If you pivoted in the right spot, you will still be aligned on your seam guide. If you did not get close enough, simply pivot back and turn the hand wheel to go forward another stitch. If you went too close to the edge, backstitch to return to the right spot. Never turn the hand wheel away from you since that tends to jam and tangle the threads.

Topstitching and edgestitching

Topstitching

Topstitching and edgestitching are used to hold seams flat and also to emphasize style lines. On fabrics that do not press well or cannot be ironed, topstitching and edgestitching are used instead to keep those seam allowances flat. You can use all-purpose or topstitch thread. A topstitch needle will make the stitching sit up a little more to show it off. Topstitching is traditionally ¼" (6 mm) away from a seam or edge while edgestitching is much closer to the edge, usually ⅛" (3 mm) or less.

TOOLS

- Zigzag foot or straight stitch foot
- Topstitch needle (optional)
- Iron and ironing board

1 Stitch the seam and press the seam allowances to one side. Press again from the right side.

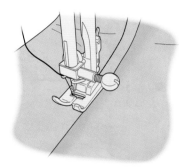

3 Lengthen the stitch length to 3 mm and set the machine to straight stitch with the needle in the center position. Topstitch, making sure to backstitch at the beginning and end.

INSIDER SECRETS

If you do not have topstitch thread, you can use two strands of all-purpose thread and thread both through the eye of a topstitch needle. Alternatively, use standard thread and a universal needle.

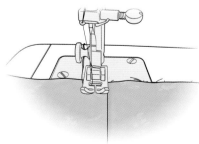

2 Align the seam on the right edge of the presser foot so that the seam allowance bulk is left of the seam.

Edgestitching

- Zigzag foot
- Topstitch needle (optional)
- Iron and ironing board

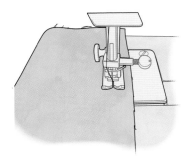

1 Stitch the seam and press the seam allowances to one side. Press again from the right side.

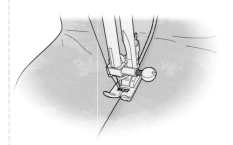

3 Lengthen the stitch length to 3 mm and set the machine to straight stitch with the needle in the center position. Edgestitch, making sure to backstitch at the beginning and end.

INSIDER SECRETS

Edgestitching is best for dressy fine garments, while topstitching has a more casual look.

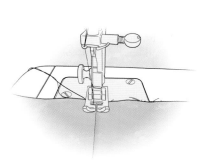

2 Align the seam with the center groove of the foot so that the bulk of the seam allowance is right of the seam.

Hems

 Topstitched hems

Topstitched hems are strong. Faced hems are ideal for curved edges such as necklines and hems. For both types, be sure to match the thread color accurately.

TOOLS

- Zigzag foot
- Universal needle sized for the fabric
- Iron and ironing board
- Seam gauge or tape measure
- Pins

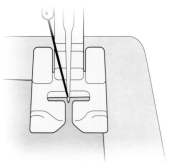

1 Press the hem to the wrong side the full amount of the hem allowance. Unfold and turn the edge under ¼" (6 mm); press again. Refold and pin the hem for sewing.

2 Working from the wrong side, line up the fold against the left edge of the presser foot and adjust the needle to the left position. Topstitch in place.

TOOLS

- Zigzag foot
- Universal needle sized for the fabric
- Iron and ironing board
- Pins
- Single-fold bias tape

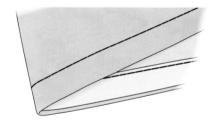

1 Place the bias tape face down against the right side of the fabric. Unfold the right edge of the bias tape so that the tape edge and hem edge are aligned, and pin securely.

3 Fold the bias tape over to the wrong side of the item to encase the raw edges and press in place with an iron.

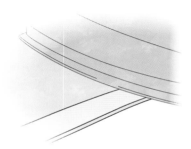

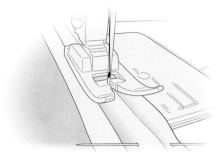

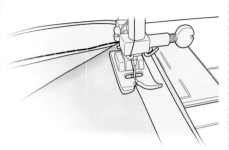

2 Stitch in the crease by lining up the crease in the center notch of the presser foot and use that as the seam guide.

4 Working from the wrong side, edgestitch the bias tape in place.

⚙ ⚙ ⚙ Bound hems

Bound hems create a superb finish to curved edges because bias tape will bend around curves. It looks especially good in contrasting colors and works well on the necklines and sleeves of garments.

TOOLS

- Zigzag foot
- Universal needle sized for the fabric
- Iron and ironing board
- Pins
- Double-fold bias tape

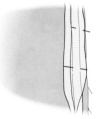

1 Double-fold bias tape has one fold that is narrower. Place the bias tape face down against the right side of the fabric with the narrow fold next to the hem edge. Unfold the top fold twice so that the edge of the bias tape and the hem are aligned, and pin in place.

3 Fold the bias tape over to the wrong side of the item to wrap the raw edges and press in place.

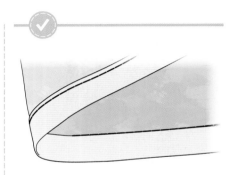

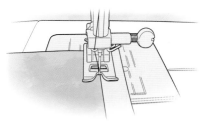

4 Working from the right side, stitch in the ditch. The fold is wider on the wrong side, so the stitches will catch the fold. On the right side the stiches will be hidden in the seam and give a clean finish.

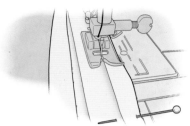

2 Stitch in the far-right crease by lining up the crease in the center notch of the presser foot and using that as the seam guide.

🔒 INSIDER SECRETS

The all-purpose foot can be used for a French seam. This is simply a self-enclosed seam. The only requirements are a basic foot, thread, needle, and iron.

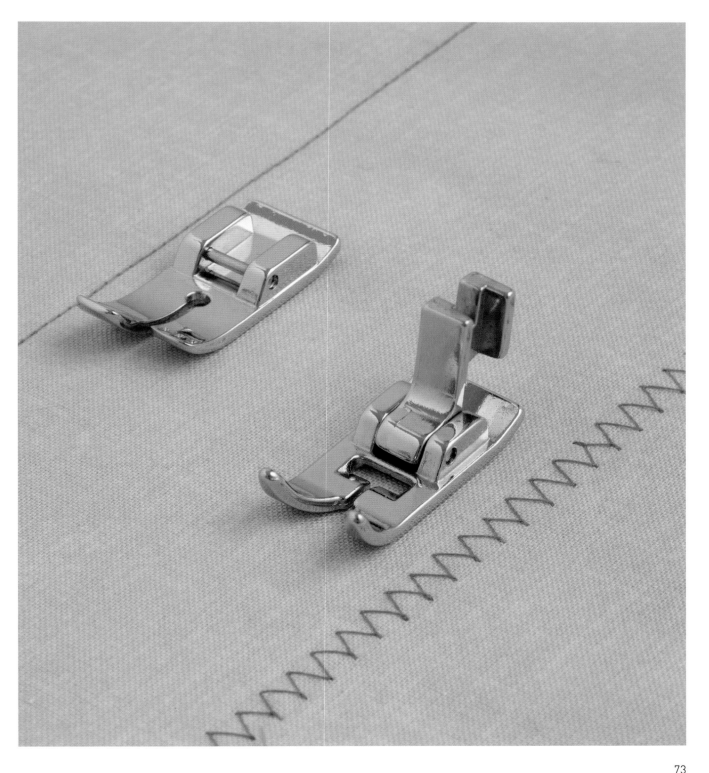

9

Zipper Feet

Types of zipper feet

The standard types of zipper feet are the narrow zipper foot, the adjustable zipper foot, and the invisible zipper foot. They all come in snap-on and screw-on varieties and are made for all machines. Your machine should come with either a narrow or adjustable foot, but invisible zipper feet are rarely included except with high-end machines.

Narrow zipper foot

AT A GLANCE

- Narrow zipper feet allow stitching close to the zipper teeth or coils
- Used with all kinds of zippers
- Has a notch on one side
- Match the needle size and type to the fabric
- Use all-purpose polyester or cotton thread

A narrow zipper foot is ¼" (6 mm) or less in width, has a small notch on one side, and can be screw-on **(a)** or snap-on **(b)**. It is designed to allow the needle to stitch very close to the zipper coils or teeth. This foot is used for stitching on all types of zippers from those with metal teeth to nylon coils to molded plastic teeth. Because there is a notch only on one side, you have to stitch down one side of a zipper and then back up the other side. This can skew fabric and pull it off grain.

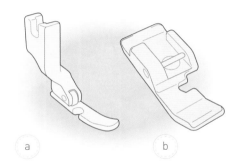

Adjustable zipper foot

AT A GLANCE

- Allows stitching close to the zipper teeth or coils
- Used with all kinds of zippers

The adjustable zipper foot can be positioned to stitch on either the left or the right of the zipper so that you can stitch down both sides of the zipper and keep the fabric on grain. It will either be a snap-on type that can be manually attached to one side or the other **(a)**, or it will have a screw to slide it left or right **(b)**. It can also be used to stitch on invisible zippers.

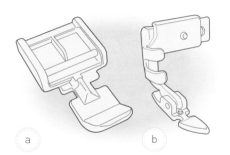

Invisible zipper foot

- Only used for invisible zippers
- Match the needle size and type to the fabric
- Use all-purpose polyester or cotton thread

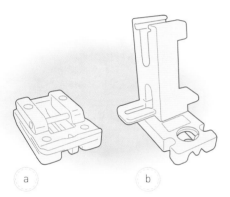

 INSIDER SECRETS

Narrow and adjustable zipper feet can be used for far more than just zippers. They are useful for making and attaching piping if you do not have a piping foot. They can also be used to stitch on trims that have edges, such as braided trims.

The invisible zipper foot has deep channels on the bottom of the foot into which the zipper coils fit. This makes it possible to stitch extremely close to the zipper coil without stitching through it. It can be snap-on (a) or screw-on (b). If the machine did not come with an invisible zipper foot and you cannot find one made for it, you can purchase a universal kit at any fabric store. The kit comes with a plastic invisible zipper foot and a low shank, slant shank, and high shank to fit any machine. It is used only for stitching on invisible zippers (c).

Using a centered zipper

Zippers are surprisingly easy to install with a zipper foot, so it is well worth mastering the technique.

TOOLS

- All-purpose foot
- Adjustable zipper foot
- Seam ripper
- Fabric marker or chalk
- Pins
- All-purpose sewing thread
- Iron and ironing board

1 Finish the seam allowances by serging, zigzag, or pinking, since this will be difficult to do after the zipper is installed.

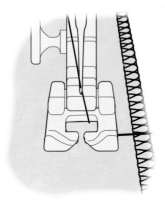

2 Pin the seam together with right sides facing. Mark the zipper stop. Stitch the seam from this mark down to the bottom of the seam, making sure to backstitch at the beginning and end.

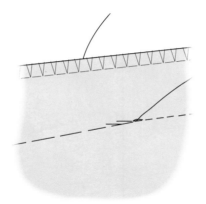

3 Adjust the stitch length to the longest length and baste the seam together from the top down to the mark. Press the seam open.

4 Working on the wrong side, place the zipper face down with the zipper coil absolutely centered on the seam. Align the zipper stop at the zipper stop mark and pin the zipper in place. On the right side, repin and remove the pins from the wrong side.

5 Install the zipper foot so that the foot is attached on the left half. Adjust the stitch length back to a standard 2.5 mm straight stitch.

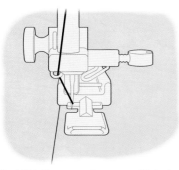

6 With the seam face up, stitch down the right side of the zipper. Line up the left edge of the foot on the seam and use that as the seam guide. At the bottom, pivot just before the zipper stop, stitch the bottom, and backstitch.

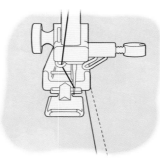

7 Now move the zipper foot over to the left and stitch down the left side of the zipper to the bottom and backstitch.

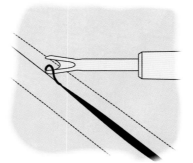

8 With a seam ripper, very carefully rip out the basting stitches and press the seam flat.

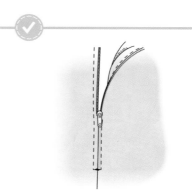

INSIDER SECRETS

Take care to match the zipper color well because it may be possible to see the zipper coils or tape. When in doubt, choose a slightly darker color because it will be less visible. Alternatively, select a zipper in a contrasting color as a design feature.

Using an invisible zipper

The invisible zipper has elegance and simplicity. It is easy to sew since there is no visible topstitching and any mistakes are hidden away.

TOOLS

- Invisible zipper foot
- Regular zipper foot
- All-purpose foot
- Pins
- All-purpose sewing thread
- Iron and ironing board

1 Finish the seam allowances by serging, zigzag, or pinking.

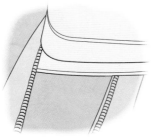

2 Unzip the invisible zipper, place it face down on the ironing board and press the coils flat.

3 Install the invisible zipper foot and check that the needle comes down right in the middle of the center hole.

4 Open the zipper and place it face down on the right side of the fabric. Line up the right edge of the zipper tape with the edge of the fabric. Slide over so that the coils are exactly ⅝" (1.5 cm) from the edge. Pin in place.

5 Line up the zipper coil in the *left* groove of the foot and stitch down until you reach the slider and cannot go any farther. The stitch will be right in the weave that you uncovered when ironing the coils flats.

6 Lay the other side of the zipper face down on the half of the garment. Again, make sure the coil is ⅝" (1.5 cm) from the edge. Line up the coil into the *right* groove and stitch down until you reach the slider.

7 Now finish the seam. Match the seam up right sides together and fold the end of the zipper tape over to the right so it does not become caught in the seam. Flatten all the materials down as much as possible. Install the regular zipper foot, and, starting about ⅛" (3 mm) up and the same distance left of the existing seam, sew about an inch (2.5 cm) or so.

8 Switch to the all-purpose foot and finish the seam with ⅝" (1.5 cm) seam allowance.

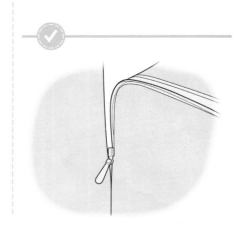

Using an exposed zipper

With an exposed zipper, the teeth or coils are visible. This is common on jackets and outerwear, but can be used as a design detail on any project.

TOOLS

- Regular zipper foot
- All-purpose foot
- Pins
- All-purpose sewing thread
- Seam ripper
- Iron and ironing board

1 Finish the seam allowances by serging, zigzag, or pinking.

2 Iron the seam allowances under to the wrong side and pin in place. Adjust the stitch length to the longest length and baste to hold the edges under.

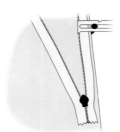

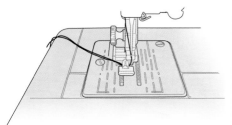

3 Install the zipper foot and adjust the stitch length back to 2.5 mm.

4 Place the left stitched seam on top of the left zipper tape and align the fold with the edge of the teeth. Pin in place. Stitch down. Repeat for the right side of the zipper.

5 Carefully remove the basting stitches with the seam ripper.

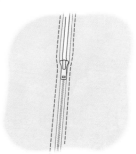

INSIDER SECRETS

You can easily shorten a zipper if you cannot find the right length in the color you need. Set the machine to a wide zigzag stitch with no length and stitch several zigzag stitches right over the coils where you want the new zipper stop to be. Cut off the excess zipper, leaving about 1" (2.5 cm) below the new zipper stop.

10

Button and Buttonhole Feet

Manual and sliding buttonhole feet

Usually mechanical sewing machines stitch a manual four-step buttonhole and computerized machines stitch an automatic one-step buttonhole. Each uses a different type of foot that comes standard with the sewing machine.

Manual buttonhole foot

AT A GLANCE

- Makes standard four-step buttonholes in any size

a

b

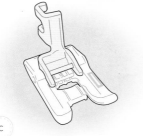

c

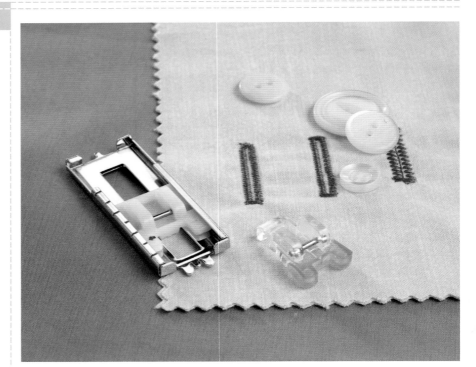

A manual buttonhole foot looks very similar to an all-purpose foot with a wide slot to allow for zigzag stitching, but on the bottom there are twin shallow grooves to allow the foot to glide over the buttonhole stitches (a). The grooves also help to keep the stitches straight and even. The manual buttonhole foot can be screw-on (b) or snap-on (c), and either plastic or metal. It can stitch a standard box buttonhole in any length.

Sliding manual buttonhole foot

- Makes four-step standard and corded buttonholes up to a fixed size

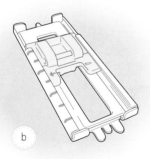

A sliding manual buttonhole has an adjustable window and markings to help to align and size the buttonholes. There are twin grooves on the bottom of the foot and also a hook on the back and a fork on the front to hold cording for corded buttonholes. Just like a manual buttonhole foot, the sliding manual buttonhole foot can be screw-on **(a)** or snap-on **(b)** and comes in both metal and plastic. It stitches standard box buttonholes **(c)** and corded buttonholes in sizes up to the length of the window.

Automatic buttonhole and button foot

Buttonholes are easy to sew with an automatic buttonhole foot. They can be simple and utilitarian or a fancy design feature. With this foot, you can sew on a button in less than a minute.

Automatic buttonhole foot

- Stitches standard, corded, keyhole buttonholes, and eyelets in one step

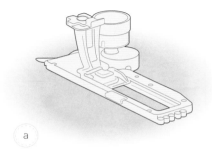

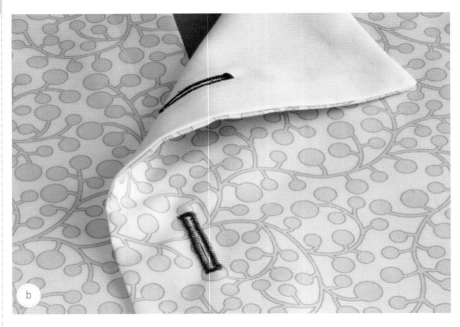

An automatic buttonhole is used on computerized and mechanical sewing machines that stitch a one-step buttonhole. It has the window and grooves of the sliding manual buttonhole foot, but also has an extension on the back where the button is inserted. The machine then automatically sizes the buttonhole to fit that button. Automatic buttonhole feet **(a)** can be snap-on or screw-on and are usually plastic. They stitch standard box **(b)** and corded buttonholes but can also stitch keyhole and rounded buttonholes, buttonholes for knit fabrics, and even eyelets, depending on the stitches offered by the machine. However, it is not possible to stitch buttonholes longer than the button slot.

Button foot

- Stitches on sew-through buttons

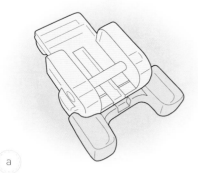

a

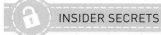

INSIDER SECRETS

Vintage sewing machines often do not have a buttonhole stitch. Instead they use an attachment called a buttonholer, which comes with metal templates that can each make a different size and type of buttonhole. If you have an older sewing machine, you can often find a compatible buttonholer on eBay or Etsy.

b

Button feet have two very short toes widely spaced that are usually coated in rubber (a). They anchor a sew-through button in place while you use a zigzag stitch to stitch it down (b). They cannot be used on shank buttons. Some button feet may have a slot to insert a pin or toothpick to create a thread shank. They can be metal or plastic, snap-on, or screw-on and are included with most machines.

Buttonholes: manual

 Manual (four-step) buttonhole

A buttonhole is a box with each of the sides made of zigzag stitches. The top and bottom are bar tacks made with a wide zigzag with no length while the sides are narrow zigzags with a very short length.

TOOLS

- Manual buttonhole or manual sliding buttonhole foot
- Tailor's chalk or fabric marker

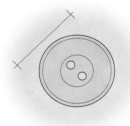

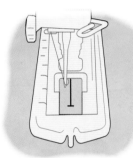

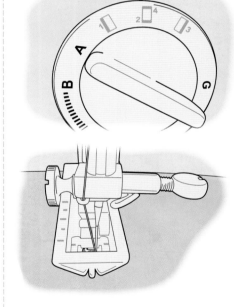

1 Mark the buttonhole on the fabric using chalk or fabric marker.

2 Adjust the stitch selector to buttonhole step 1 and the stitch length to 0.5 mm. Place the buttonhole foot on the sewing machine and adjust the slider so that the marking is perfectly framed in the window.

3 Stitch down the left side of the buttonhole until you reach the bottom. If you are using a sliding foot, the window sliding will close as you stitch down toward the bottom. Make sure that the last stitch is on the left side of the zigzag and that the needle is out of the fabric.

4 Adjust the selector to buttonhole step 2 and sew five stitches so that you finish on the right side. The stitch will automatically adjust to a wider and shorter zigzag. Make sure the needle is out of the fabric when you finish the last stitch.

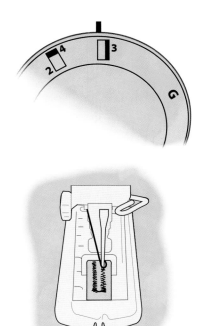

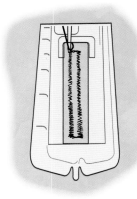

7 To lock in the stitch, adjust the selector to straight stitch, change your stitch length to 0 mm, and sew three to four stitches. Trim off the threads.

5 Adjust to buttonhole step 3 and stitch back up to the top. The stitch will be the same as step 1 but you will be sewing in reverse. As you sew, the window will slide back open. Make sure the last stitch is on the right and that the needle is out of the fabric.

6 Adjust the selector to step 4 (often the same as step 2) and sew five stitches. Make sure the needle is out of the fabric when you finish the last stitch.

INSIDER SECRETS

- How big should a buttonhole be? It should be the diameter of the button, plus the height, plus ⅛" (3 mm). The additional ⅛" allows a little bit of extra room so that the buttonhole does not come out too small. The height is added because tall buttons need the buttonhole to open wider than flat buttons.

- You can adjust the stitch length on the buttonhole. While a shorter stitch looks good, be aware that some fabrics do not feed easily and they may jam if the stitch length is too short.

Buttonholes: automatic

 Automatic buttonhole

Automatic buttonholes will all come out identical and the technique is very fast.

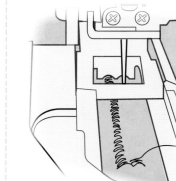

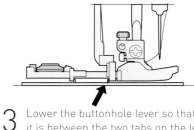

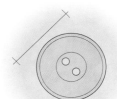

TOOLS

- Automatic buttonhole foot
- Tailor's chalk or fabric marker

1 Insert the button into the slot on the back of the buttonhole foot. This will slide the window to the correct size for that button. Install the foot on the sewing machine.

2 Mark the buttonholes on the fabric with chalk or a fabric marker.

3 Lower the buttonhole lever so that it is between the two tabs on the left side of the foot.

4 Adjust the pattern selector to buttonhole stitch.

5 Position the foot so that you are starting at the beginning. Press the foot pedal and start stitching. The machine will stitch one side, across the top, back down, and then across the bottom all in one step. At the end, the machine will do a couple of lock stitches to secure the thread.

If you are stitching a buttonhole on a thin or stretchy fabric, apply interfacing to the wrong side of the fabric before you stitch the buttonholes. It will provide support to prevent the fabric from stretching and distorting.

Fancy buttonholes

 Keyhole buttonholes

Keyhole buttonholes are used on tall buttons since an automatic buttonhole foot does not adjust for button height. Flat buttons can use either a box or rounded buttonhole.

TOOLS

• Automatic buttonhole foot

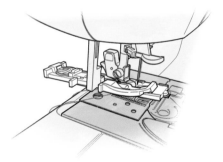

1 Insert the button into the slot on the back of the buttonhole foot to slide the window to the correct size. Install the buttonhole foot and lower the buttonhole lever between the two tabs on the side of the foot.

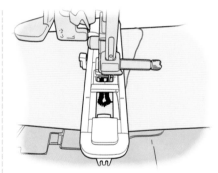

2 Select the keyhole buttonhole stitch and position the foot so that you are starting at the beginning. The machine will stitch half the rounded end, up one side, across the top, back down, and then the other rounded half all in one step.

Corded buttonholes

Corded buttonholes are stitched on top of thick thread. They have a raised look and are used on knits or plush fabrics where a standard buttonhole would disappear into the fabric.

TOOLS

- Automatic buttonhole foot or sliding buttonhole foot
- Cord, topstitch thread, or embroidery floss
- Tailor's chalk or fabric marker

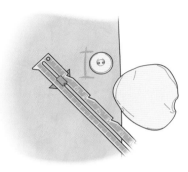

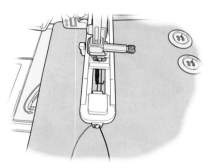

1 Mark the buttonhole on the fabric.

3 Lower the foot, select a buttonhole stitch, and sew the buttonhole as normal. Pull the cord forward and clip off the ends.

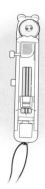

2 Slip the cord over the hook on the back of the foot. Bring it forward to the front and secure through the fork on the front.

Stitching buttons and making buttonholes

 ## Stitching on buttons by machine

Stitching on buttons is a quick job when done by machine using a button foot.

TOOLS

- Button foot
- Darning plate (optional)
- Pin or toothpick
- Handsewing needle

1 Adjust the stitch length to 0 mm (or drop the feed dog or install the darning plate) and adjust the stitch selector to the widest zigzag. Install the button foot. Align the button in position, then lower the presser foot down so that the holes are between the toes. Slide the pin between the button and foot. This creates slack in the thread to make a thread shank.

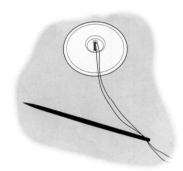

2 Using the hand wheel, manually walk the needle down into one hole and back up and down into the other hole to ensure it goes cleanly through the holes. You may need to adjust the stitch width. When it is correct, use the foot pedal and zigzag back and forth five to six times. If you have a four-hole button, rotate the button to do the other set of holes.

3 Leave long thread tails when you have finished stitching. Thread them through a hand needle, pull through to the back of the button and wrap around the thread a couple of times to make a shank. Then pull the threads to the wrong side of the fabric, tie off, and clip.

 ## INSIDER SECRETS

Use a contrasting thread color to make the buttons a design detail. On four-hole buttons, stitch across the holes as an X, as two parallel lines, or sew around the sides to form a square.

Cutting open a buttonhole

TOOLS

- Seam ripper
- Straight pin
- Fabric punch or awl

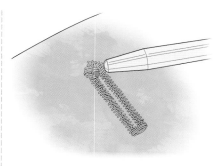

1   Place a pin through the top bartack. Starting from the bottom bartack, carefully slide the seam ripper up through the center of the buttonhole. The pin will form a stopper and will prevent you from slicing too far.

2   Use the fabric punch to cut open the round end of a keyhole buttonhole or eyelet.

INSIDER SECRETS

Apply a drop of seam sealant to the buttonhole and let it dry before you cut it open to prevent the threads from fraying.

11 Hemming

Types of hemming feet

Basic hems can be stitched using the standard all-purpose foot, but some hemming techniques require a special foot to achieve truly professional results.

Blind hem foot

- Creates an invisible hem for dressy garments

- Suitable for medium- to heavyweight fabrics

- Appropriate needle sizes are 75/11 or 80/12 universal

- Use all-purpose polyester or cotton thread in a matching color or use invisible thread

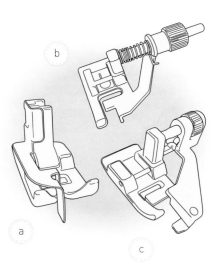

A blind hem (also known as an invisible hem) adds a classy touch on trousers, skirts, and dresses if you want to avoid visible topstitching on the right side. It is commonly seen on suit trousers and skirts. A well-stitched blind hem should be practically invisible from the right side and all you should see is a tiny stitch every ½" (1.3 cm) or so. On the wrong side you will see a series of zigzag stitches (d). A blind hem works well on a variety of fabric types, making it suitable for clothing as well as heavier work such as sewing curtains.

Blind hem feet come in a few varieties and may be screw-on (a) or snap-on (b and c). One excellent type has an adjustable bar that can be moved right next to a fold of fabric when stitching blind hems, and you can also use it as a guide for topstitching and decorative stitching (b and c). You can also obtain a blind hem foot that has a metal guide in the center for accuracy; the fold of the fabric fits snugly against it (a).

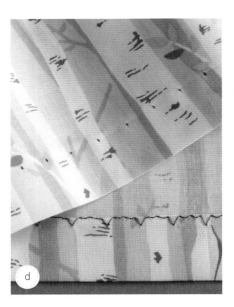

INSIDER SECRETS

You can also use the blind hem foot for topstitching, edgestitching, and decorative stitches.

Rolled hem foot

- Creates narrow rolled hems that are 2 mm to 6 mm wide

- Best used for lightweight to medium-weight fabrics

- Appropriate needle sizes are 70/10 or 80/12 universal or Microtex

- Use all-purpose polyester or cotton thread in a matching color

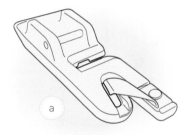

INSIDER SECRETS

You can use the rolled hem foot as a guide for sewing on narrow trims. Simply slip the trim through the scroll and it will feed through as you sew, making it easy for you to stitch it on straight.

The rolled hem foot (a) is used to quickly and easily turn a narrow amount of fabric over twice and stitch it down in one smooth motion (b). Without a rolled hem foot, you would need to spend a large amount of time pressing tiny amounts of fabric. Rolled hem feet are also called narrow hemming feet, or sometimes hemmers, and are available in different sizes. The most common size is 2 mm but they are also available in 4 mm or 6 mm. The finished hem width is directly related to the size of the front scroll and the groove on the foot's bottom.

You will frequently see a rolled hem on scarf edges and napkins, but also on the hems of dresses and skirts and along ruffle edges. A rolled hem works best on sheer or lightweight fabrics such as chiffon, georgette, batiste, voile, lawn, and charmeuse.

Most machines come with a 2 mm rolled hem foot. High-end machines may come equipped with the larger sizes, but you can purchase a hem foot separately. Hem feet are available in both snap-on and screw-on styles for low-shank, high-shank, and slant-shank machines.

Blind hem

This hem, also called an invisible hem, is used to avoid visible top stitches on the right side of the fabric. It works best on relatively straight edges.

TOOLS

- Blind hem foot
- Sewing gauge
- Pins
- Iron and ironing board

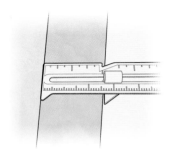

1 Press the hem to the wrong side the full amount of the hem allowance. Now fold the hem back so that ¼" (6 mm) of the raw edge extends out.

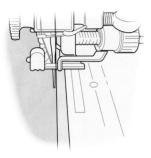

3 Using the hand wheel, walk the machine until the needle swings to far-left zigzag. The needle should just barely catch the fold. Using the hand screw, adjust the bar on the foot so that it comes right up against the fold. This is the seam guide.

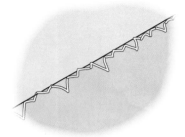

5 Unfold the hem and press it flat. On the wrong side you will see a zigzag edge. From the right side you should barely be able to see a tiny stitch every ½" (1.3 cm) or so.

 INSIDER SECRETS

If you see a big stitch on the right side, then you stitched too much onto the fold. If it does not catch at all, then you stitched off the fold. The blind hem can be hard to master, so take your time and practice.

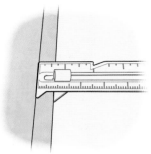

2 Install the blind hem foot on the machine. Select the blind hem stitch and a stitch length of 2.5 mm.

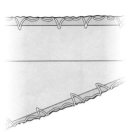

4 Start stitching. The big zigzag will catch just a thread of the fold, and the little zigzags will finish the raw edge and prevent fraying.

Rolled hem

A rolled hem is a very pretty finish on delicate fabrics and is perfect for hems and sleeves on dresses and blouses.

TOOLS

- Tools
- Rolled hem foot
- Sewing gauge
- Pins
- Iron and ironing board

1 Iron the hem to the wrong side ⅛" (3 mm) and then iron under another ⅛" (3 mm).

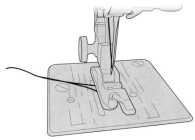

2 Install the rolled hem foot on the sewing machine and select a basic straight stitch with a length of 2.5 mm.

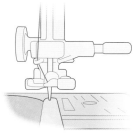

3 Take a couple of stitches on the hem edge and with the needle down in the fabric, lift the presser foot.

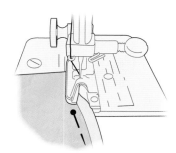

4 Use a pin to gently guide the hem into the scroll of the rolled hem foot and then lower the presser foot.

5 Finish stitching the hem, going slowly and gently easing the fabric into the scroll.

INSIDER SECRETS

If the fabric is very slippery, try spraying it with spray starch and ironing it dry. The starch will stabilize the fabric and make it easier to guide into the scroll. The starch will wash out after the garment is complete, but be sure to do a test on a scrap of the fabric first to make sure the starch will not stain.

Top-, edge- & coverstitch hem

✿◌◌ Topstitching and edgestitching

It can be very difficult to stitch perfectly straight topstitching and edgestitching when the seam guides are covered by the fabric. Using a blind hem foot provides you with a guide that is easy to position and see.

TOOLS

- All-purpose foot
- Blind hem foot
- Iron and ironing board

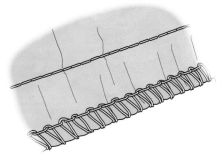

1 Stitch the seam and finish the raw edges by serging, zigzag, or pinking.

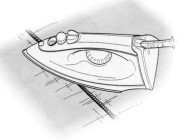

2 Press the seams and turn right side out. You will be working from the right side.

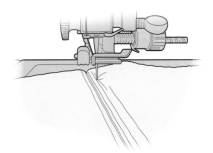

3 Remove the all-purpose foot and replace with the blind hem foot. Place the fabric under the foot, and, using the hand wheel, lower the needle down into the fabric where the stitching will go.

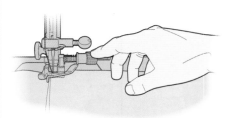

4 Using the hand screw, adjust the bar on the foot so that it comes right up against the seam or edge. This will be the seam guide and you should watch it as you stitch. Topstitch the seam.

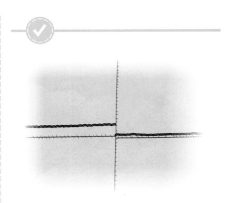

🔒 INSIDER SECRETS

You can topstitch hems as well as seams.

Coverstitch hem

You do not need a coverstitch machine to hem knits professionally. You can do a faux coverstitch on a general sewing machine using a twin needle and a basic straight stitch. The bobbin thread zigzags back and forth between the two needles and the seam can stretch.

TOOLS

- Blind hem foot
- Twin needle
- Sewing gauge
- Pins
- Iron and ironing board

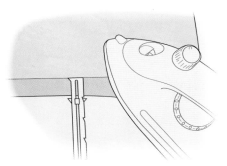

1 Press the hem under to the wrong side the full amount of the hem allowance and pin in place.

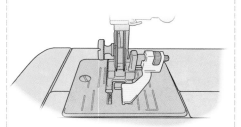

3 Install the blind hem foot on the machine and set the machine to a straight stitch with a length of 2.5 mm.

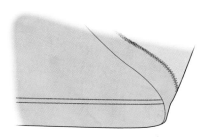

5 Stitch the hem, backstitching at the beginning and end.

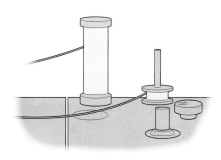

2 Insert the twin needle into the sewing machine and thread the machine with two threads, making sure that the threads do not tangle as you thread them.

4 Working from the right side, line up the fabric so that the twin needle will stitch right on the edge. Adjust the bar on the foot so it is right on the edge of the underlayer.

 ### INSIDER SECRETS

Rather than buying a second spool of thread for the top, simply wind a second bobbin and use that as the second thread.

12

Ruffles and Gathers

Types of ruffling and gathering feet

Most sewists create gathers by stitching two rows of basting stitches and then pulling on the bobbin threads to draw up the fabric. Rufflers and gathering feet can do this more quickly and accurately. You can use the gathering and ruffling feet to embellish fabric with shirring, make gathered, ruffled, or pleated edges, or make trims.

Gathering foot

AT A GLANCE

- Creates soft gentle gathers
- Suitable for light- to medium-weight fabrics
- Appropriate needle sizes are 75/11 or 80/12 universal
- Use all-purpose thread orelastic thread

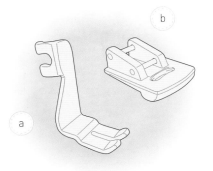

A gathering foot (also called a shirring foot) has a wide, flat base at the front and a raised base at the back. Only the front portion comes in contact with the feed dog and this creates the soft, gathered effects when stitching. The foot can have a single hole for straight stitching or a wide hole to allow zigzag stitches. Gathering feet come in single and double varieties, and the double foot has a slot on the left side. The double foot is the more versatile, because you can gather fabric and stitch it to another fabric in one operation. Gathering feet are metal and can be snap-on **(b)** or attached to a low, slant **(a)**, or high shank.

You can use a gathering foot to ease in fullness on sleeve caps, gather skirts and stitch them to a waistband, or gather trims **(c)**. Gathering feet work well with lightweight fabrics, but not so well with heavy or stiff fabrics. You can also use them with elastic thread for elastic shirring. You can increase the degree of fullness by lengthening the stitch. Always do a test stitch on a scrap of the fabric to determine the amount of fullness you will achieve with a particular stitch length.

INSIDER SECRETS

If you have a gathering foot with a wide hole, try using a twin needle to do two rows of gathering stitches simultaneously. This helps to keep the fabric from twisting as it gathers.

Ruffler attachment

- Creates evenly spaced tucks every one, six, or twelve stitches
- Works with all weights of fabric
- Appropriate needle sizes are 75/11 or 80/12 universal
- Use all-purpose polyester or cotton

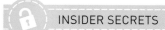

INSIDER SECRETS

To figure out how long to cut the ruffle, always do a test swatch. Cut a strip of fabric 10" (25 cm) long and stitch it with the gathering foot or ruffling foot. Measure it to work out the ratio. For example, if it comes out 7" (18 cm) long, it is 30 percent shorter, so you will need to cut the fabric 30 percent longer than the required length.

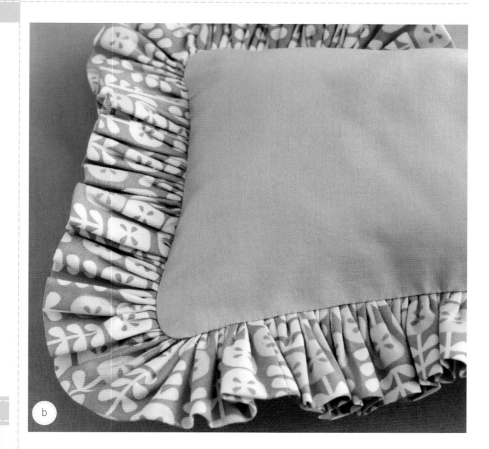

A ruffler is a large metal attachment used to create evenly spaced tucks and pleats. It has a fork that hooks over the needle bar and a toothed blade on the bottom that pushes small tucks of fabric under the needle. You can adjust it to create a tuck every one, six, or twelve stitches and you control this setting on the top of the attachment. You can control the depth of the tuck with a small screw on the front. Rufflers are nearly always screw-on **(a)** and you need to use one designed for the type of shank on your machine.

Rufflers can be used to ruffle a length of fabric. They can also ruffle one fabric and stitch it to a base fabric with one pass, or even ruffle a fabric, stitch it to a base, and stitch on a top facing simultaneously. Rufflers are excellent for ruffling ribbons for trims or to create ruffled trims from fabric **(b)**. They work successfully with all weights of fabric.

Gathering fabric

This will create soft gathers in lightweight fabrics.
Use it to gather an edge or create a ruffled hem.

TOOLS

- Double gathering foot
- All-purpose thread

1 Install the gathering foot on the machine and set the machine to a straight stitch with a stitch length of 3 mm.

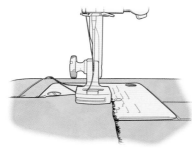

2 Put the single piece of fabric to be gathered on the bottom of the foot and line up the edge on the right edge of the foot.

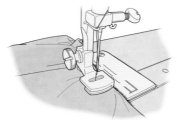

3 Backstitch and then start stitching. You will see the fabric start to gather up as you stitch. Backstitch at the end.

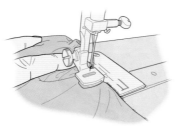

4 If you want more gathering, push your finger against the back of the foot as you stitch.

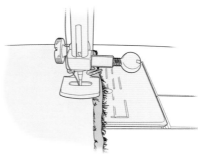

5 To gather and stitch in one operation, the fabric to be gathered goes on the bottom and the other fabric goes in the slot.

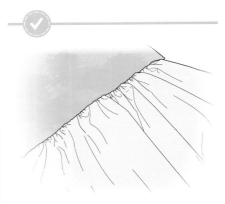

INSIDER SECRETS

The seam allowance will be smaller on the non-gathered fabric, so use a fabric marker or tailor's chalk to mark a line on the bottom fabric to match up the layers and then stitch.

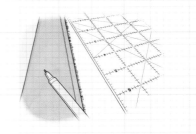

Pleating fabric

A ruffler attachment makes pleats rather than gathers and can be used on all weights of fabric.

TOOLS

- Ruffler attachment
- All-purpose thread

1 Install the ruffler attachment on the machine. Make sure the hook is attached to the needle bar.

2 Select the pleat spacing by adjusting the selector on the front. One tuck per stitch will be a very full ruffle while one tuck every twelve stitches will be flatter.

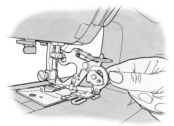

3 Select the depth of the tuck by adjusting the screw and sliding the dial: eight will be the deepest tuck. On some rufflers you turn the screw to the right to deepen the tuck.

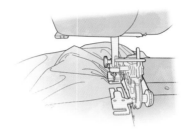

4 Slide the fabric under the toothed ruffler blade, lower the presser foot, and start stitching.

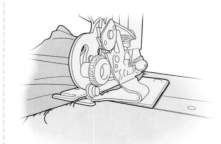

5 To ruffle and stitch at the same time, insert the base fabric under the flat bottom blade.

6 To also stitch on a facing, insert the facing fabric through the top guide.

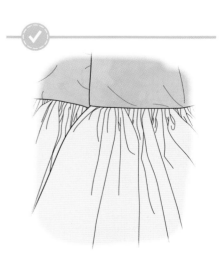

Shirring fabric

Shirring is the forming of parallel rows of stitching that gather the fabric slightly and create fullness.

- Single or double gathering foot
- Fabric marker or tailor's chalk
- Quilting guide
- All-purpose thread

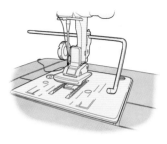

1 Install the gathering foot and quilting guide and set the machine to a straight stitch with a length of 3 mm.

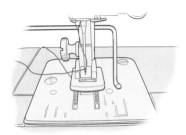

3 Determine the distance between the rows and adjust the quilting guide to that measurement.

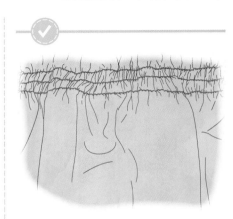

2 Mark a line on the fabric for the first row of stitching.

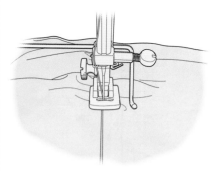

4 Stitch along the first line and use the quilt guide to stitch the subsequent rows.

INSIDER SECRETS

If you want the fabric to stretch, use elastic thread in your bobbin and all-purpose thread through the needle. The more rows you stitch, the greater the gathering effect.

Ruffles and Gathers

Ruffled and pleated trims

Using a ruffler attachment, you can easily and quickly make designer trims for a fraction of the price of ready-made trims.

TOOLS

- Ruffler attachment
- Flat ribbon such as satin or grosgrain
- Matching all-purpose thread

1 Install the ruffler attachment on the machine. Make sure the hook is attached to the needle bar.

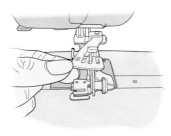

2 Select the pleat spacing by adjusting the selector and select the depth of the tuck by adjusting the screw.

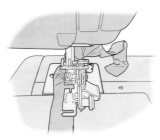

3 Slide the ribbon under the toothed ruffler blade, lower the presser foot, and start stitching along one edge.

4 To ruffle and stitch to another ribbon at the same time, insert the base ribbon under the flat bottom blade using one of the guides on the bottom of the ruffler.

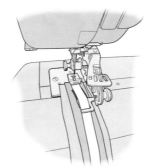

5 To also stitch on a top ribbon, insert the ribbon through one of the top guides.

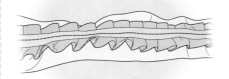

INSIDER SECRETS

Try layering the trims. Ruffle a grosgrain ribbon down the middle and stitch onto a wider satin ribbon. You can also ruffle several ribbons together. Experiment with various widths of trims for different effects.

Ruffles and Gathers

13

Seam Finishes

Types of seam finishing feet

Many sewists believe they need a serger to finish seam allowances. However, a variety of feet make it easy to finish seam allowances neatly and professionally using a general sewing machine.

Overcast/overedge foot

- Pin holds fabric edges flat while stitches form over the pin
- Suitable for all fabrics
- Match the needle size and type to the fabric
- Use all-purpose polyester or cotton thread

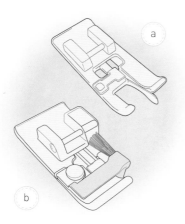

The overcast, or overedge, foot has a small pin **(a)** or brush **(b)** that holds the fabric edges down flat to prevent them from curling under and a blade to the right to act as a seam guide. The needle will zigzag over the pin or through the brush. You can stitch along the edge with the right side of the zigzag going off the edge to prevent the fabric edges from raveling **(c)**. You can also use this foot to stitch and finish a seam in one step by using an overcast stitch. The effect is similar to the look created with a serger. The overcast foot is usually metal and can be snap-on, and there are screw-on versions for all shank types. Most new machines come with an overcast foot but if yours didn't, they are easy to source.

Never use a straight stitch or an elastic (multistitch zigzag) stitch with this foot because the needle will hit the center pin and break.

Felling foot

- Rolls the top seam allowance under to create a topstitched seam

- Best used with medium to heavy fabric weights

- Appropriate needles are 90/14 or 100/16 universal, denim, or topstitch

- Use all-purpose thread or topstitch thread

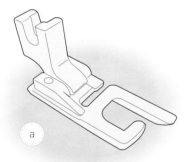

INSIDER SECRETS

Use a heavy topstitching thread and a topstitch needle to create a ready-to-wear look. Gold topstitching thread is traditionally used for denim, but try other colors to create a unique look.

A flat-felled seam features a topstitched seam allowance and is very strong because it is stitched twice (b). It is commonly seen on jeans and workwear and often has the topstitching in a contrasting thread color. You can stitch this type of seam with an all-purpose foot, but a felling foot makes it easier and gives you consistently perfect results. The foot has a large scroll or extended toe that rolls the top layer of seam allowance under to cover the bottom seam allowance. You use the right edge of the foot as a seam guide to topstitch a consistent distance from the edge. The felling foot can be metal or plastic and comes in screw-on (a) or snap-on versions for low, high, or slant shank types. It is rarely included with a machine and needs to be purchased separately.

Side cutter

- Trims, finishes, and stitches seams in one step
- Works best for light- to medium-weight fabrics
- Match the needle size and type to the fabric
- Use all-purpose polyester or cotton thread

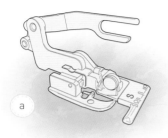

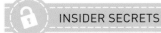 INSIDER SECRETS

You cannot use the automatic needle threader once the side cutter is attached on most versions. Thread the needle before you attach the side cutter.

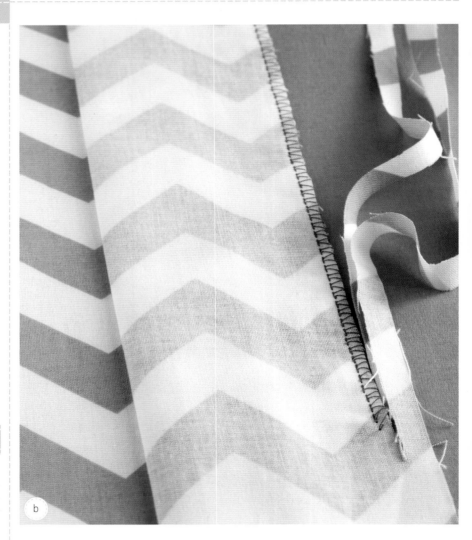

The side cutter acts as a serger attachment that stitches, trims, and finishes seams in one step. It has an upper and lower knife to trim off the fabric edges, a pin to hold the edges flat, and uses zigzag or overcast stitches to finish seam allowances **(b)**. The side cutter has a bar or hook that goes over the needle bar; it works to move the knives with each stitch. It is a big attachment and comes in snap-on or screw-on low-shank, slant- shank, and high-shank versions **(a)**. The side cutter needs to be purchased separately.

Stitch in the ditch foot

- Has a large center blade that acts as a guide
- Works with all weights of fabric
- Match the needle type and size to the fabric
- Use all-purpose polyester or cotton thread

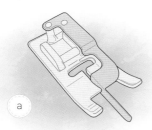

INSIDER SECRETS

You can also use a stitch in the ditch foot for ditch quilting and traditional ditch stitching on waistbands, collars, and cuffs.

The stitch in the ditch foot has a fixed center blade between the toes. The blade rides along the join of a seam or along an edge to act as a seam guide for topstitching and edgestitching, but is also extremely helpful for bound seams (b) and French seams. This foot is metal with a large metal blade and can be snap-on (a) or screw-on for all shank types. Higher-end machines may include one of these feet, but they are readily available for all machine makes and models.

Overcast & flat-felled seams

 Overcast seam

The overcast seam finish looks like a serger stitch and prevents the cut edges from raveling.

TOOLS

- Overcast foot
- All-purpose foot
- Pins

1 Install the all-purpose foot and set the machine a straight stitch with a stitch length of 2.5 mm.

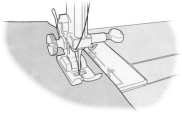

2 With fabrics pinned right sides facing and the raw edges aligned, stitch a basic straight seam, backstitching at the beginning and end. Trim the thread tails.

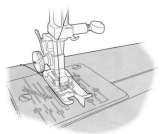

3 Install the overcast foot and set the machine to a zigzag or overcast stitch with a stitch length of 2.5 mm.

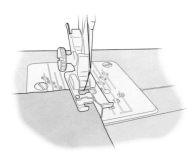

4 Align the raw edges along the blade and lower the presser foot.

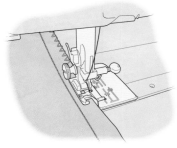

5 Overcast the edges and trim your thread tails at the end.

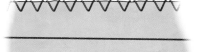

INSIDER SECRETS

To finish and stitch in one step, use an overcast stitch and a ¼" (6 mm) seam allowance.

Flat-felled seam

A flat-felled seam is a lapped topstitched seam and is very strong. It is best used on straight seams and is reversible to look neat from both the front and back.

TOOLS

- Felling foot
- Scissors
- Pins
- Iron and ironing board

1 Install the felling foot and set the machine to a straight stitch with a stitch length of 2.5 mm.

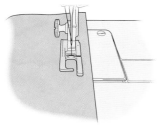

2 With the fabrics wrong sides facing and the raw edges aligned, stitch a basic straight seam, backstitching at the beginning and end. Trim the thread tails.

3 Press open the seam allowances and then trim the left seam allowance down to ¼" (6 mm).

4 Lengthen the stitch length to 3 mm.

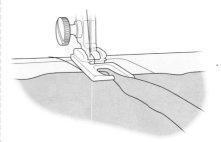

5 Roll the top larger seam allowance around the scroll so that it covers the smaller seam allowance and then lower the presser foot.

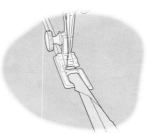

6 Line up the seam on the right edge of the foot and stitch the seam down, backstitching at the beginning and end.

INSIDER SECRETS

Use a zigzag or decorative embroidery stitch for the final step to add a decorative look.

Serged seam

A serged seam is neat and very durable and can also stretch, making it ideal for stretch knits.

1 Install the side cutter attachment on the machine. Make sure the hook is attached around the needle bar.

2 Select an overcast stitch or zigzag stitch and a stitch length of 2.5 mm.

3 Align the fabrics with the right sides facing and the raw edges together. At the end, make a cut in the fabric approximately ¾" (19 mm) long.

4 Place the fabrics under the foot and pin with the cut ¾" (19 mm) part over the guide plate and next to the cutting blades.

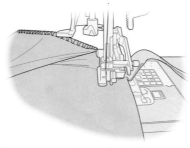

5 Lower the foot and stitch the seam, backstitching at the beginning and end.

INSIDER SECRETS

You must cut in the ¾" (19 mm) at the beginning or the attachment will not work. Clean the blades after use to prevent lint buildup.

French seam

A French seam is an enclosed seam that looks beautiful on the wrong side and like a standard seam from the right side. It is ideal for sheer and lightweight fabrics.

TOOLS

- All-purpose foot
- Overcast foot
- Pins
- Scissors
- Iron and ironing board

1 Install the all-purpose foot and select a straight stitch with a stitch length of 2.5 mm.

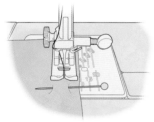

2 With your fabrics wrong sides facing, stitch a ⅜" (1 cm) seam, backstitching at the beginning and end.

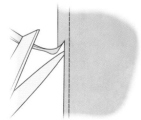

3 Trim the seam allowances down to ⅛" (3 mm) and press the seam allowances to one side. Fold back so that the right sides are facing and press again so that the seam is right on the edge.

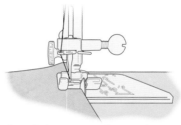

4 Install the overcast foot on the machine and align the blade on the fabric edge.

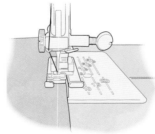

5 Move the needle to the left position. Stitch a ¼" (6 mm) seam, backstitching at the beginning and end, for a total ⅝" (1.5 cm) seam allowance.

INSIDER SECRETS

French seams do not work well for thick fabrics because the multiple layers create too much bulk. Try a bound seam for heavy wool and canvas fabric.

Bound seam

A bound seam (sometimes called a Hong Kong finish) wraps the raw edge of the seam allowance with another fabric. This is an excellent option for bulky fabrics and looks gorgeous on unlined garments or on facing edges.

TOOLS

- All-purpose foot
- Stitch in the ditch foot
- Pins
- Iron and ironing board
- Double-fold bias tape
- Iron and ironing board

1 Install the all-purpose foot on the machine and select a straight stitch with a 2.5 mm length.

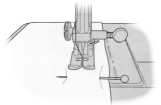

2 With the fabrics right sides facing, stitch a ⅝" (1.5 cm) seam, making sure to backstitch at the beginning and end. Press the seam open.

3 Unfold the bias tape and align the edge of the smaller fold with the edge of the seam allowances.

4 Stitch in the crease, backstitching at the beginning and end.

5 Wrap the bias tape around the fabric edge to the back of the seam allowance.

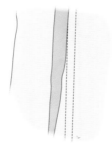

6 Install the stitch in the ditch foot and align the blade right on top of the seam of the bias tape. Stitch along the seam, catching the bottom fold of the bias tape. Repeat for the other seam allowance.

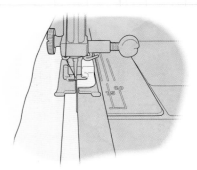

14

Embroidery and Quilting

Types of embroidery and quilting feet

Embroidery and quilting feet help to feed fabric easily and also provide good visibility for maximum creativity. They allow any general sewing machine to be an inspirational dynamo. Most of these feet are included only with high-end machines.

Satin-stitch foot

AT A GLANCE

- Groove on bottom rides over dense stitching

- Match the needle size and type to the fabric and thread

- Appropriate for all fabric types

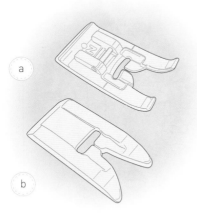

A satin-stitch foot looks like a standard zigzag foot **(a)** except it has a deep groove on the bottom **(b)** to accommodate the buildup of dense stitches when using satin stitch or decorative embroidery stitches **(c)**. It can be metal or plastic and has a well-defined center-front mark for use as a seam guide. Satin-stitch feet can be snap-on or screw-on for all shank types.

Appliqué foot

- Clear foot for maximum visibility
- Closed toe supports fabric
- Match the needle size and type to the fabric and thread
- Suitable for all fabrics

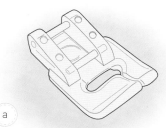

INSIDER SECRETS

Satin stitch is simply a zigzag stitch with a very short length that covers a base fabric. It is used for appliqué (**b**), monograms, and decoration.

The appliqué foot is very similar to the satin-stitch foot, except that it is completely clear for even better visibility and has a closed toe to provide good support to the fabric when stitching. It is a smaller foot for better maneuvering around tight curves and has a guide mark on the front. It is usually snap-on **(a)**.

Open-toe foot

- Open toe gives excellent visibility
- Match the needle size and type to the fabric and thread
- Suitable for all fabrics

INSIDER SECRETS

The appliqué, satin-stitch, and open-toe feet are interchangeable. They can all be used for appliqué, monograms, and decorative stitches (b). The appliqué foot is best for tight curves, while the open-toe foot and satin-stitch foot are perfect for straight lines and loose curves.

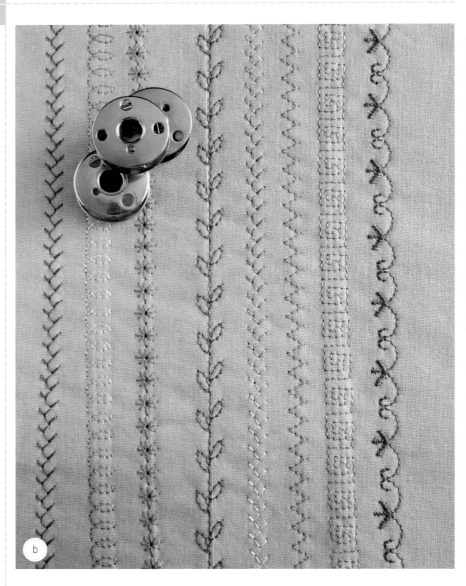

The open-toe foot provides an unobstructed view of your work while sewing since there is no bridge between the toes, and the long toes provide good traction against the feed dog. Like the appliqué and satin-stitch feet, it has a groove to permit dense stitches to pass underneath. Open-toe feet can be metal or plastic and can be obtained in snap-on (a) or screw-on versions.

¼" (6 mm) patchwork foot

- Has a ¼" (6 mm) right toe and markings for ⅛" (3 mm) and ¼" (6 mm) pivot turns

- Use for patchwork and topstitching

- Appropriate needles are 75/11 or 80/12 universal

- Use all-purpose polyester or cotton thread

The ¼" (6 mm) foot is also called a patchwork or piecing foot and has a narrow right toe with a guide that is exactly ¼" (6 mm) from the center needle position **(a)**. It may also have a ⅛" (3 mm) marking on the right toe and ¼" (6 mm) and ⅛" (3 mm) markings on the sides for perfectly placed pivot turns. This foot is used for piecing quilt tops, patchwork, topstitching, and any situation where absolute accuracy is paramount **(b)**. It can be plastic, metal, snap-on, or attached to a shank.

Free-motion embroidery foot

- Use for embroidery, monograms, quilting, and darning

- Spring-mounted foot used with an embroidery hoop

- Must lower the feed dog or cover it with a darning plate

- Use all-purpose thread or rayon embroidery thread

The free-motion embroidery foot is also known as a darning foot. This tall, slender foot is spring mounted and has a bar or hook that sits over the needle bar––. The hook and spring work in place of the feed dog as your hands move the fabric around. It can have an open or closed toe that is made of metal or plastic. An open toe allows for excellent visibility while you are stitching, while a closed toe gives more support to the fabric around the stitching. Free-motion feet are screw-on, and you can obtain them for low **(a)**, high, or slant-shank machines.

Free-motion embroidery feet are excellent for embroidery, monograms **(b)**, quilting, stippling, and darning. They can use straight, zigzag, or decorative stitches. When using the free-motion embroidery foot, ensure that you keep your hands moving in unison with the sewing machine to create even stitches.

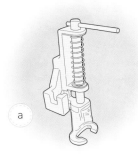

Flower attachment

- Maximum radius of 1" (2.5 cm)
- Fits low-shank machines only
- Match the needle type and size to the thread
- Use all-purpose or novelty threads

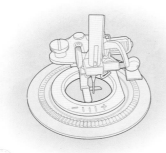

a

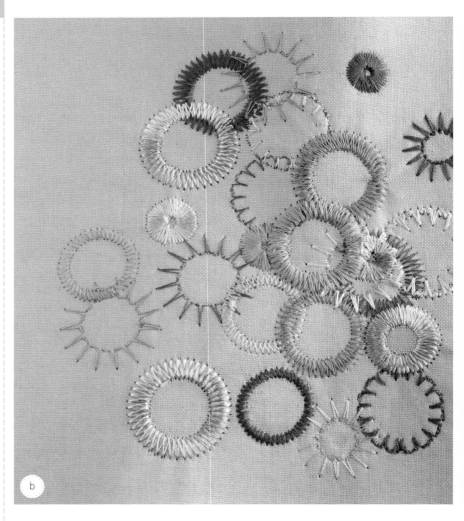

b

The flower attachment **(a)** is a spring-action foot that works with the needle bar to rotate fabric in a circle. It has a notched plastic wheel around the foot that moves the fabric around one step with each stitch. The flower attachment makes three sizes of circles ranging from approximately ⅜" (1 cm) diameter up to a 1" (2.5 cm) diameter circle. You can use any kind of stitch, such as straight, zigzag, or embroidery stitch, and it will stitch these in a circle to make a flower shape **(b)**. You can also use a twin needle to create concentric circles. You can overlap circles and create your own embroidered fabric and can experiment with novelty threads, for example, variegated, metallic, and rayon threads. The flower attachment foot is available in screw-on and snap-on versions, only for low-shank machines.

Circle attachment

- Has a pin that rotates fabric in a circle
- Use for decorative stitches and trims
- Match the needle type and size to the fabric and thread
- Use with any foot

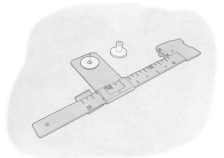

INSIDER SECRETS

Use a wash-away or tear-away stabilizer to prevent soft fabrics from bunching up when using either a flower or circle attachment. You can also hoop the fabric to keep it taut.

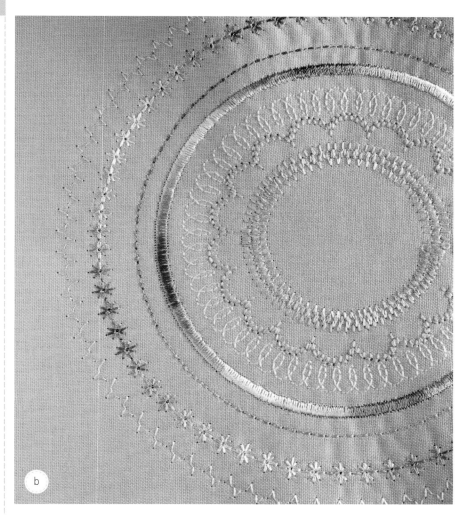

The circle attachment clamps or screws to the sewing-machine bed and has a very sharp pin that holds the fabric in place (a). As you sew, the fabric will spin in a perfect circle around the pin. You can adjust the size from a small 1" (2.5 cm) diameter circle up to a 12" (30 cm) diameter circle. You can use any foot and any type of stitch with this attachment. It is excellent for stitching decorative stitches in a circle (b), but also for stitching trims in a circle. Try it with beaded trims or ribbons or use it to stitch appliqués. Circle attachments can vary in appearance and you need to use one designed for your machine.

Appliqué

Appliqué is the application of patches of fabric to a base fabric. It can be purely decorative or used to hide holes and stains.

1 Apply fusible interfacing to the wrong side of the appliqué fabric, following the manufacturer's instructions for iron temperature and time.

2 Using the fabric marker or chalk, draw the appliqué shape on the wrong side of the fabric.

3 Cut out the appliqué.

4 Place the appliqué face up on the fabric and pin it in place or use basting spray to hold it in place.

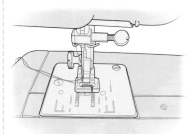

5 Install the satin-stitch or appliqué stitch on the machine and select a zigzag stitch with a width of 4 mm and a length of 1 mm.

Embroidery and Quilting

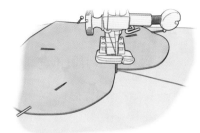

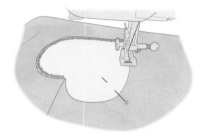

6 Turn the hand wheel on the machine until the needle is on the right side of the zigzag and position the fabric so that the needle comes down just outside the edge of the appliqué.

7 Satin stitch all the way around the appliqué, leaving long thread tails at the beginning and end instead of backstitching.

8 Using a handsewing needle, pull the top thread tails through to the wrong side of the fabric and hand tie off.

INSIDER SECRETS

- You can also appliqué with other decorative stitches. Some machines are equipped with blanket stitches and reverse appliqué stitches.

- Since you are drawing on the back of the appliqué fabric, the image should be reversed. This is especially important to remember when drawing letters.

Decorative stitches

Most sewing machines include a variety of decorative stitches. These include zigzag and triple-zigzag, embroidery, smocking, and cross-stitch. Experiment with different widths and lengths.

TOOLS

- Satin-stitch or open-toe foot
- Quilting bar
- Decorative thread (rayon, metallic, embroidery, or variegated)
- Embroidery needle or metallic needle
- Wash-away or tear-away stabilizer
- Iron and ironing board

1 Apply the stabilizer to the wrong side of the fabric, following the manufacturer's instructions.

2 Select a decorative stitch and adjust the length and width as desired.

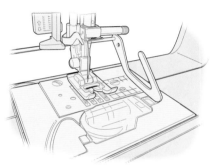

3 Install the satin-stitch or open-toe foot and insert the quilting bar into the shank.

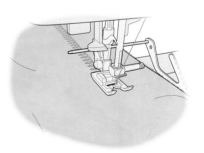

4 Stitch one row of decorative stitches across the entire length of fabric.

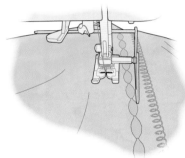

5 Select the next type of stitch. Align the quilting bar on the first row of stitches and then stitch the next row.

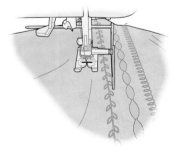

6 Continue sewing rows of stitches until the desired look is achieved. Remove the stabilizer, following the manufacturer's recommendations.

Embroidery and Quilting

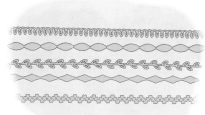

- While you can use all-purpose thread for decorative stitching, this is the ideal opportunity to try out some fancy threads, such as variegated, glow-in-the-dark, or metallic threads.

- If you want a portion of a garment embellished, cut a block of fabric first, embellish it, and then cut out the pattern piece.

Monograms

A monogram can be made from simple block letters or complex scripts.

TOOLS	
• Free-motion embroidery foot	• Wash-away stabilizer
• Letter template	• Fabric marker
• Decorative thread (rayon, metallic, embroidery, or variegated)	• Embroidery hoop
	• Darning plate (optional)
	• Iron and ironing board
• Embroidery needle or metallic needle	• Handsewing needle

1 Design the monogram. Either use the computer to print out a letter or use a purchased template.

2 Trace the letter on a layer of stabilizer using the fabric marker.

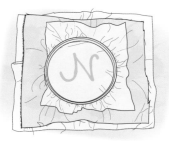

3 Hoop the fabric between two layers of stabilizer, making sure it is evenly stretched and taut. The stabilizer with the letter should be on top.

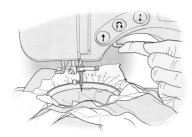

4 Slide the hooped fabric under the foot. You may need to push up on the presser-foot lifter for extra-high clearance to get the hoop under the foot.

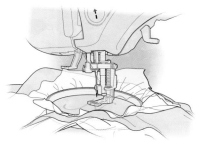

5 Install the free-motion embroidery foot, making sure the bar is aligned properly above the needle bar, and install the embroidery or metallic needle.

6 Lower the feed dog or cover it with the darning plate and set the machine to a wide zigzag stitch.

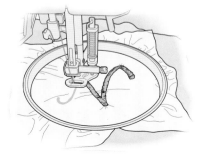

7 Start stitching. Since you don't have the feed dog to move the fabric, use your hands to move the hoop as you stitch. The spring on the foot will go down with each stitch and then come back up so you can move the fabric.

8 Leave long thread tails, and using a hand needle, pull the top threads through to the wrong side of the fabric and hand tie them off. Remove the stabilizer according to the manufacturer's instructions.

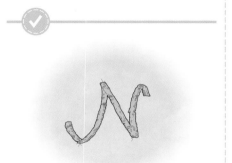

INSIDER SECRETS

Block letters are easiest, so practice with those first and then try fancier script letters. Some high-end sewing machines have a stitch regulator that times the stitch with the movement of the hoop to keep the stitches even.

Free-motion embroidery

This is a great way to add embellishment to fabrics. Be creative and design as you go, or draw out a design and stitch along the lines. This technique is similar to painting, but with thread.

TOOLS

- Darning plate or the ability to lower the feed dog
- Wash-away or tear-away stabilizer
- Embroidery hoop
- Tailor's chalk, fabric marker, or transfer paper
- Handsewing needle

1 Following the manufacturer's instructions, apply the stabilizer to the wrong side of the fabric.

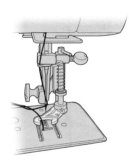

3 Install the free-motion embroidery foot, making sure the bar is aligned properly above the needle bar.

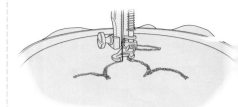

5 Hoop the fabric, making sure it is evenly stretched and taut.

2 Draw the design on the right side of the fabric using the chalk, marker, or transfer paper.

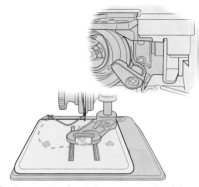

4 Lower the feed dog or cover it with the darning plate.

6 Slide the hooped fabric under the foot. You may need to push up on the presser-foot lifter for extra-high clearance to get the hoop under the foot.

Embroidery and Quilting

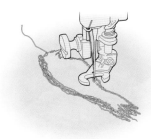

7 Start stitching. Since you do not have a feed dog to move the fabric, use your hands to move the hoop as you stitch. The spring on the foot will go down with each stitch and then come back up so you can move the fabric.

8 Leave long thread tails, and using a hand needle, pull the top threads through to the wrong side of the fabric and hand tie them off. Remove the stabilizer according to the manufacturer's instructions.

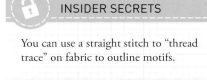

INSIDER SECRETS

You can use a straight stitch to "thread trace" on fabric to outline motifs.

Patchwork and piecing

Piecing is the process of stitching together small pieces of fabric to make a larger block of fabric. Accuracy is the key to ensure that the final block is the desired size, and the ¼" (6 mm) foot makes this straightforward. Below is a simple placemat design.

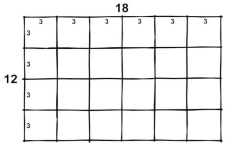

1 Decide on the finished size of the placemat and draw it out on a piece of paper. This one is an 18" by 12" (46 by 30 cm) rectangle.

2 Draw lines to divide up the rectangle into simple blocks. Here there is a line every 3" (8 cm) to give a total of 24 squares. Measure the side of the blocks and add a ½" (1.3 cm) seam allowance to each block to account for the ¼" (6 mm) seam allowance on each side.

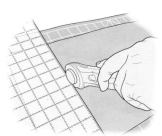

3 Using the rotary cutter, mat, and quilt ruler, cut out the fabrics according to your plan.

4 Make small piles of the fabrics for each row with the fabrics stacked in the order you will stitch them.

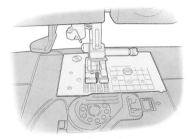

5 Install the ¼" (6 mm) foot on the machine and select a straight stitch with the needle in the center position and a length of 2.5 mm.

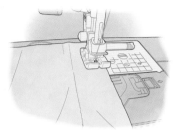

6 Stitch the first pieces together with the raw edges of the fabrics right against the ¼" (6 mm) guide on the foot.

7 Continue stitching all the squares together for the first row and then press the seam allowances to one side.

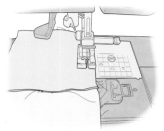

8 Stitch the blocks for the remaining row and press the seam allowances. Then finish the placemat top by stitching all the rows together with a ¼" (6 mm) seam allowance.

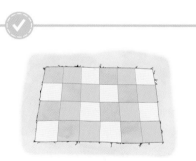

INSIDER SECRETS

Continuous sewing is a great time saver when piecing many pieces of fabric. At the end of one seam, stitch one stitch off the edge. Stitch right on to the next section without raising the presser foot. Continue stitching as many pieces as you need. When you have finished, simply cut the chain to separate the sections and then press the seam allowances.

Flowers

A flower attachment makes it easy to embellish anything with flowers, and you can be creative with novelty threads.

1 Apply the stabilizer or interfacing according to the manufacturer's directions. Use the marker or chalk to draw the placement of the flowers to provide a guide to follow.

2 Install the flower attachment, making sure the bar or hook is over the needle bar, then lower the feed dog or attach a darning plate.

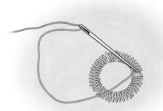

4 Leave long thread tails and use a hand needle to pull them to the wrong side; hand tie them off.

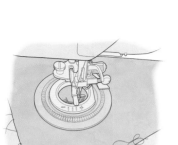

3 Select a wide zigzag stitch and place the fabric under the foot. Lower the foot and start stitching. The fabric will rotate one turn with each stitch.

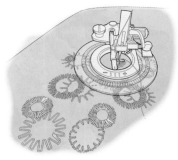

5 Continue stitching the flowers until you have the look you want.

Embroidery and Quilting

There are many ways to use the flower attachment. Try stitching a smaller flower inside a larger flower or overlap the flowers to give a shadow effect.

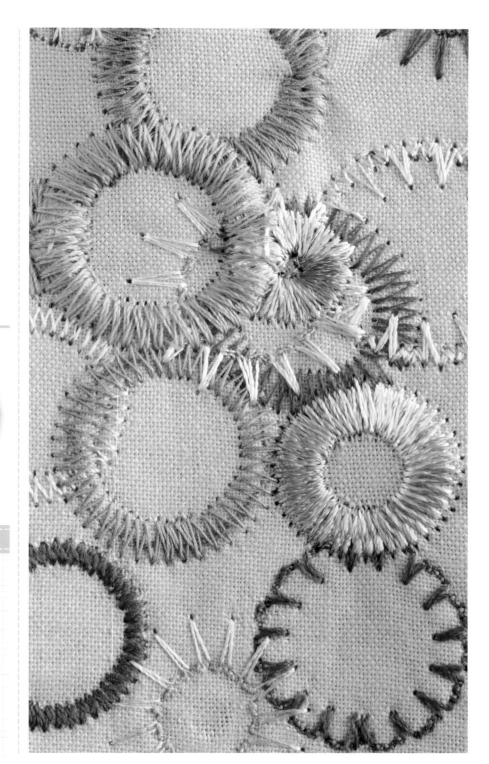

Circles

The circle attachment makes perfect circles and can be used for simple stitches using an all-purpose foot or any other type of foot designed for specific fabrics or tasks.

TOOLS

- Circle attachment
- Tear-away stabilizer or lightweight fusible interfacing
- Fabric marker or tailor's chalk
- Iron and ironing board
- Presser foot of your choice

1 Apply the stabilizer or interfacing to the wrong side of the fabric according to the manufacturer's directions. Use the marker or chalk to mark the center of the circle.

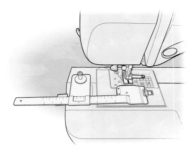

2 Attach the circle attachment to the sewing machine, following the machine instructions. Set the guide for the size of circle desired.

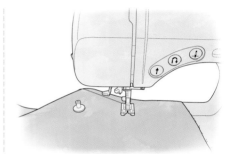

3 Remove the stopper from the pin and insert the pin through the center mark on the circle from the wrong side.

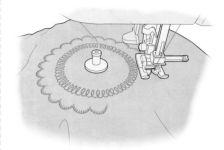

4 Install the presser foot, lower the foot, backstitch, and start stitching.

Try using the walking foot with the circle attachment for perfectly stitched quilted circles. Use it with a satin-stitch or appliqué foot for appliquéd circles, or try it with a beading and pearl foot to stitch around trims in a circle.

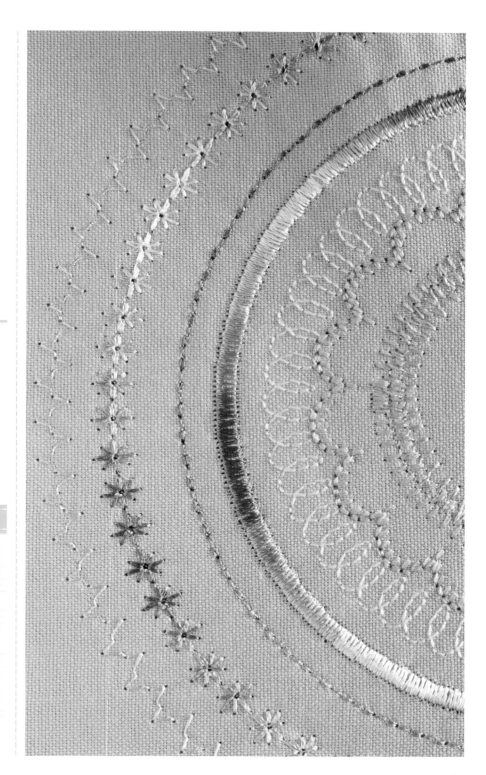

15

Specialty Fabrics

Types of specialty fabric feet

Teflon feet glide across sticky fabrics, such as vinyl, while walking feet evenly feed fabrics and keep plaids and stripes aligned. Roller feet easily stitch across uneven layers and knit feet prevent stretch knits from rippling.

Teflon foot

AT A GLANCE

- Easily glides over fabrics that stick to a standard foot

- Available in zigzag, straight stitch, or zipper variations

- Match the needle size and type to the fabric

- Use all-purpose polyester thread

A Teflon foot is a white plastic presser foot made of thermoplastic polymer. This nonstick foot is used for fabrics and materials that tend to stick to the bottom of a standard metal presser foot **(c)**. The Teflon foot is ideal for laminated fabrics, oilcloth, vinyl, plastic, and leather since it will easily glide across these fabrics and keep the stitches even. Most Teflon feet are a standard zigzag style **(a)**, but you can also buy Teflon straight stitch and zipper feet. They are available as a snap-on style or attached to a shank for low shank, slant shank, or high shank machines **(b)** and usually need to be bought separately.

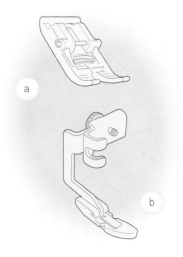

INSIDER SECRETS

You can get Teflon strips that stick on to the bottom of a standard metal presser foot. If using these, dedicate a foot to them so that you will not need to remove the strips.

Roller foot

- Rolls over heavy fabrics and uneven thicknesses
- Good for sticky and slippery fabrics
- Match the needle size and type to the fabric
- Use appropriate thread for the fabric and needle type

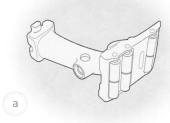

a

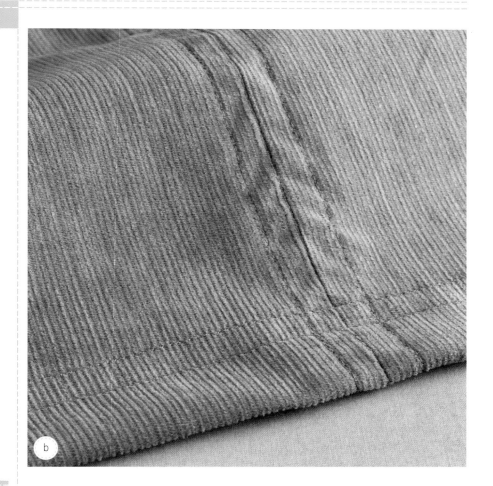
b

INSIDER SECRETS

When stitching on leather, vinyl, or oilcloth try using a leather needle. This needle will make a clean hole through these materials to make even and beautiful stitches.

A roller foot has textured metal wheels or rollers and is designed to feed the upper layer of fabric through evenly with the bottom layer. It can be used on fabrics such as leather, plastic, and suede that tend to stick to the bottom of a standard foot. The roller foot is also suitable for fabrics that are thick **(b)** or have a pile and it is good for velvet and denim. It can easily climb over uneven layers and is good for hemming heavy fabrics. The textured wheels are perfect for slippery fabrics such as satin or charmeuse. The roller foot has a wide slot to allow for zigzag stitches and is usually clear for good visibility. It may have a front and back roller or have wheels **(a)** at each corner. The foot may be snap-on or attached to a shank **(a)**. Roller feet nearly always need to be purchased separately.

Knit foot

- Designed for even feeding of lightweight and silky fabrics

- Snap-on foot for low-shank machines

- For knits, use a 70/10 ballpoint or stretch needle and polyester thread

- For silks, use a 70/10 Microtex needle and cotton thread

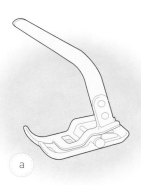

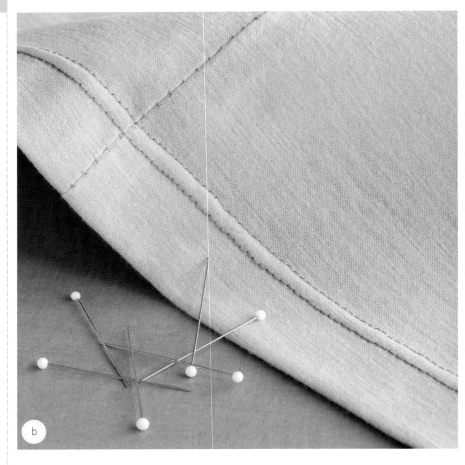

INSIDER SECRETS

Although the knit foot is designed for low-shank machines, many sewists have been able to use it successfully on high-shank snap-on machines as well.

The knit foot **(a)**, also known as a tricot foot, is used when sewing lightweight and flimsy knit fabrics or silky fabrics to prevent the fabric from stretching and rippling **(b)**. The foot has a grip that holds the fabric down as the needle penetrates it and a bar that hooks over the needle bar. As the needle bar goes up, it lifts the lever on the knit foot, which pulls up the grip and allows the feed dog to advance the fabric forward for the next stitch. The foot has a wide hole for zigzag, decorative, and twin needle stitching. It is a snap-on foot designed for low-shank machines only. The knit foot usually has to be purchased separately.

Walking/even-feed foot

- Has an upper feed dog to evenly feed layers of fabric

- Good for sticky, slippery, stretchy, or thick fabrics

- Match the needle type and size to the fabric

- Use all-purpose polyester or cotton thread

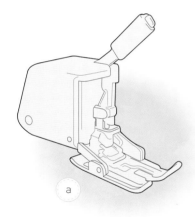

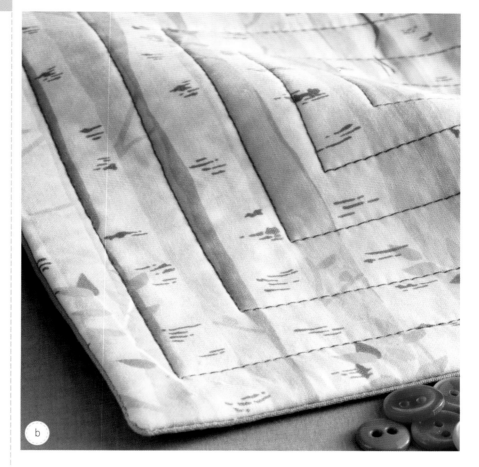

INSIDER SECRETS

Some sewing machines come with a built-in even-feed mechanism. You simply push a button on the shank and an upper feed dog engages.

Seam slippage is when the top layer of fabric ends up longer than the bottom layer. The walking foot is an attachment that has an upper feed dog to feed layers of fabric through the machine at the same speed as the bottom layers. It has an arm or hook that connects to the needle bar, and when the needle bar pulls the needle out of the fabric, it moves the upper feed dog. Walking feet are wonderful when precision sewing is essential and they are used to keep plaids and stripes aligned and for piecing patchwork. They can also be used for fabrics that are difficult to feed, such as plastic, vinyl, and knits and also for thick fabrics, including denim and faux fur. They are perfect for quilting through lofty batting **(b)**. The walking foot has a wide needle hole to allow for zigzag stitches and twin needles and has a slot on the back in which to insert a quilting bar. It is a screw-on foot designed for low-shank **(a)**, slant-shank, and high-shank machines. The walking foot is often included with high-end machines and machines marketed to quilters.

Sewing leather and vinyl

Leather, vinyl, oilcloth, and laminates are easy to stitch with a Teflon foot. Some sewists use a walking foot or a roller foot but those feet can leave impressions on very soft leathers.

TOOLS

- Teflon foot
- Leather needle size 80/12 or 90/14
- Seam creaser
- Mallet (for thick fabric)

1 Install the Teflon foot on the machine and set the machine to a straight stitch with a stitch length of 3 mm.

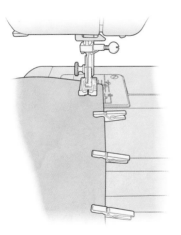

2 Place the fabrics right side facing and raw edges aligned. Stitch the seam, backstitching at the beginning and end.

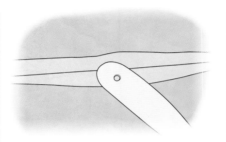

3 Turn right side out and push the seam allowances open or to one side with the seam creaser. (An iron would damage the material.)

4 From the right side, use the mallet to gently pound the seam flat if the material is extremely heavy and does not lie flat.

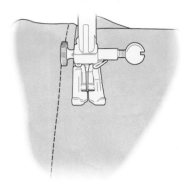

5 Topstitch the seam allowances flat.

Do not use pins when working with leather, oilcloth, or similar fabrics because they will leave permanent holes. Instead, use paper clips or clothespins to hold the layers together. You could also try using basting tape or even a glue stick.

Sewing knits and velvet

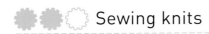 **Sewing knits**

It is easy to stretch out knit fabrics when stitching them with an all-purpose foot. A knit foot or walking foot will keep the seams flat and ripple free.

TOOLS

- Knit or walking foot
- Ballpoint needle or stretch needle
- Twin needle (optional)
- Seam gauge
- Pins

1 Install the knit or walking foot on the machine, align the hook over the needle bar, and set the machine to a stretch stitch with a stitch length of 2.5 mm.

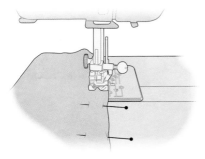

2 Pin the fabrics right sides facing, and with the raw edges aligned, stitch a basic seam, backstitching at the beginning and end. Trim the thread tails.

3 To hem knits, press the seam allowance to the wrong side, using the seam gauge to measure accurately.

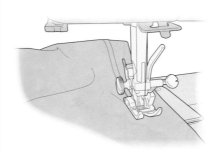

4 Stitch the hem as close to the raw edge as possible using a stretch stitch or a twin needle for a coverstitch.

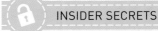

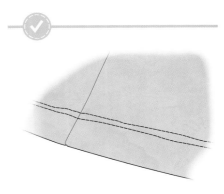

INSIDER SECRETS

Good stretch stitches include a narrow zigzag, overcast, stretch straight (the triple straight stitch), or elastic stitch. Be careful not to stretch the fabrics as you sew. Let the machine feed the fabrics.

Sewing velvet

Velvet and other pile fabrics such as corduroy can have massive seam slippage since the fabric layers tend to shift away from each when stitching. A roller foot or walking foot keeps the layers aligned and feeding evenly.

TOOLS

- Roller or walking foot
- Microtex sharp needle
- Seam creaser
- Pins

1 Install the roller or walking foot and select a straight stitch with a seam allowance of 2.5 mm.

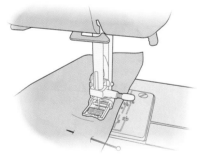

2 Install a Microtex needle. With the fabrics pinned right sides facing and the raw edges aligned, stitch a straight seam, backstitching at the beginning and end. Trim the thread tails.

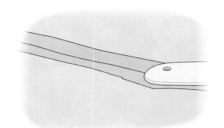

3 Turn right side out and press open the seam allowances with the seam creaser.

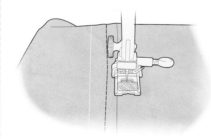

4 Topstitch or edgestitch the seams to hold the seam allowances flat.

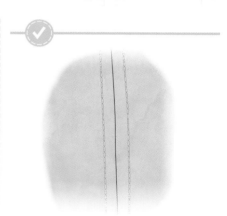

INSIDER SECRETS

Be very careful when ironing pile fabrics because you can permanently crush the fibers and leave a shine mark. Always press from the wrong side and place a scrap piece of velvet or a terry-cloth towel on the ironing board to create a bed for the fibers to settle into. You can also purchase a special ironing surface called a Velva Board or a needle board.

Quilting lofty fabrics

Quilting is stitching batting between layers of fabric, and most batting is very thick. A walking foot keeps these layers from shifting and a quilting bar gives you a visible guide to follow.

TOOLS

- Walking foot
- Quilting needle
- Quilting bar
- Safety pins or hand needle and thread

1 Install the walking foot on the machine, aligning the hook over the needle bar, and select a straight stitch with a 3 mm length.

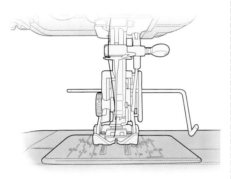

2 Insert the quilting bar on the back of the walking foot and adjust it to the desired distance.

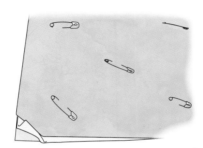

3 Use safety pins to secure the batting between the fabrics or use a hand needle and thread and baste together.

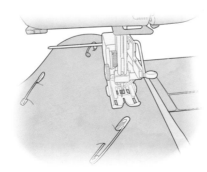

4 Install a quilting needle. Stitch the first line of stitching through all of the layers.

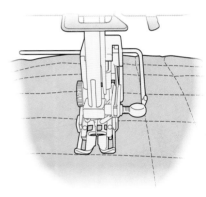

5 Line up the quilting bar on the first line of stitching and stitch the next row. Continue until all the rows of stitching are complete.

You can stitch parallel rows of quilting stitches using a straight seam or you can use decorative stitches. Experiment on a scrap to see what looks best. All-purpose sewing thread works well for this stitching, but you can also try rayon embroidery thread or novelty threads.

Sewing patterned and slippery fabrics

 Sewing plaids and stripes

When sewing plaids and stripes it is imperative that they stay aligned to achieve a professional result.

TOOLS

- Walking foot
- Universal needle
- Pins
- Iron and ironing board

1 Install the walking foot on the machine, aligning the hook over the needle bar, and select a straight stitch with a 2.5 mm length.

2 Fold back the seam allowance on one piece to expose the plaid or stripe.

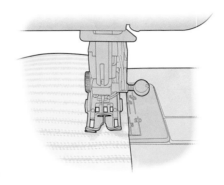

4 Install a universal needle. Stitch the seam, backstitching at the beginning and end.

3 Place the fabrics with right sides facing, making sure to line up the pattern precisely, and pin securely.

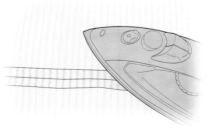

5 Turn right side out and press open the seam allowances.

INSIDER SECRETS

It is extremely important to match plaids and stripes when cutting them out or they will never match when sewn. Pick a corresponding notch on each pattern piece and place it on the same part of the plaid. By matching the notches, you are also matching the plaid.

Sewing slippery fabrics

Slippery fabrics such as chiffon or charmeuse can slide and stretch as you sew them. A knit or walking foot keeps the layers from sliding away from each other.

TOOLS

- Knit foot or walking foot
- Microtex sharp needle
- Pins
- Iron and ironing board
- Press cloth

1 Install the knit foot on the machine and select a straight stitch with a 2.5 mm length.

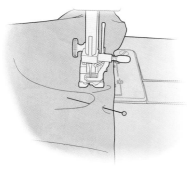

2 Install a Microtex needle. With the fabrics pinned right sides facing, stitch the seam, making sure to backstitch at the beginning and end.

3 Turn right side out and press open the seam allowances. Slip a press cloth under the seam allowances to prevent them from leaving an impression on the fabric.

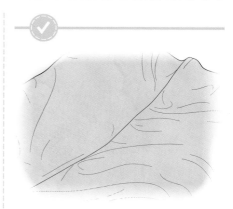

INSIDER SECRETS

Slippery fabrics can be very difficult to cut accurately. Try spraying the fabric with spray starch and ironing it dry. The starch will stiffen and stabilize the fabric, making it easy to cut. The starch will wash out, but always test on a scrap first to make sure it will not stain.

16

Trims and Embellishments

Trim and embellishment feet

Trim and embellishment feet range from simple piping and welting feet to fancy fringe feet. Each foot is designed for a specific task; for example, piping is using for garments; welting is used for home décor. Some trim and embellishment feet are exclusive to certain sewing-machine brands.

Cording foot

AT A GLANCE

- Has between three and seven cord guides
- Used with zigzag and decorative stitches to couch down cord
- Use all-purpose, invisible, or decorative thread

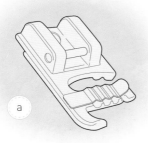

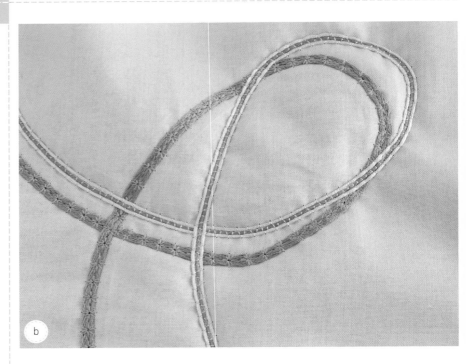

A cording foot has three **(a)** to seven holes or slots to hold and guide cords under the foot as you use a zigzag stitch to couch them down. You can couch over embroidery floss, fine yarn, metallic thread, or any other type of cord **(b)**.

Use a basic zigzag stitch, three-step zigzag, or decorative stitch, ensuring the stitch has enough width to cover the cords. You can use all-purpose or novelty thread, or use invisible thread.

Pintuck foot

- Creates evenly spaced pintucks
- Best used with light- to medium-weight fabric
- Use with a twin needle
- Use all-purpose polyester or cotton thread

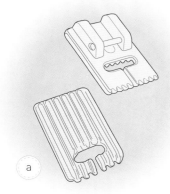

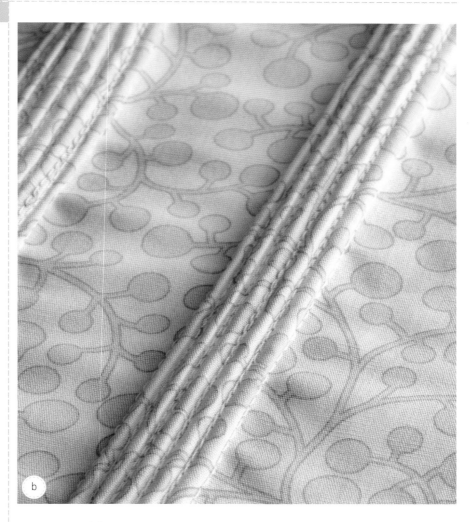

A pintuck foot **(a)** has three to nine channels on the bottom and is used to create consistent and evenly spaced pintucks on light- to medium-weight fabrics **(b)**. It is always used with a twin needle; the width of the twin needle will determine the depth of the tuck. Make sure you use a twin needle appropriate to the fabric. After you stitch one tuck you move it into an adjoining channel and stitch the next tuck—the tucks will be perfectly spaced.

Piping foot

- Has a single deep channel on the bottom
- Use a universal needle sized for the fabric type
- Use all-purpose polyester or cotton thread

a

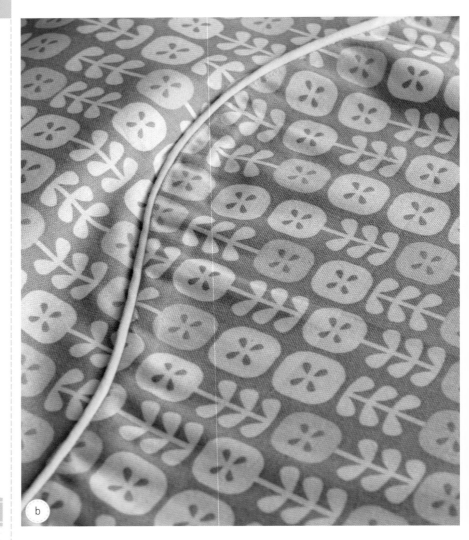

b

INSIDER SECRETS

The piping foot with a wide hole can be used interchangeably with most beading and pearl feet.

A piping foot has a single narrow deep groove on the bottom through which to feed piping. It is usually clear plastic and comes with various width channels for different sizes of piping **(b)**. The ⅛" (3 mm) size **(a)** is the most useful. It may have a single hole for straight stitching or a wide hole for adjustable needle positions and zigzag stitching.

Welting foot

- Has a single or double deep channel on the bottom

- Use a universal needle sized for the fabric type

- Use all-purpose polyester or cotton thread

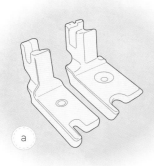

Piping is using for garments while welting is used for home décor (**b**). Technically, they are the same thing, but piping is smaller than welting.

Welting feet look similar to piping feet but they have a larger channel on the bottom ranging from ⅛" (3 mm) **(a)** up to ½" (1.3 cm) in diameter and are made of metal. The channel is left of center and the foot has a small needle hole for straight stitch only. There are also double welting feet with two channels side by side.

Sequin and ribbon foot

- Has a guide to feed flat trims such as ribbon and sequins
- Use with all weights of fabric
- Match the needle size and type to the fabric and thread
- Use all-purpose, novelty, or invisible thread

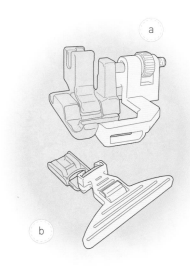

INSIDER SECRETS

You can purchase a ribbon attachment that screws onto the needle plate on the sewing machine. It has an adjustable channel to work with different widths of trims.

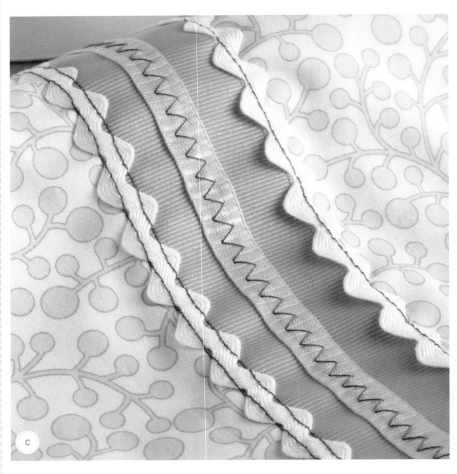

The sequin and ribbon foot has a wide, flat guide on top through which to feed flat trims such as ribbon, elastic, or sequin trim. The guide will determine the size of the trim you can use. Some sequin and ribbon feet only accommodate trims up to 3/16" (5 mm) wide, while others work with wider trims. The latter have a wider slot for the needle to accommodate various needle positions. On most sequin and ribbon feet there is a dial to adjust the feed slot left or right to position it precisely on the fabric. Some ribbon feet have a single slot (a) but others have multiple slots (b) so you can feed several ribbons simultaneously and stitch them in layers. You can use this foot with basic straight stitching or with zigzag or decorative stitches. Novelty threads such as rayon or metallic threads add pizazz while invisible thread disappears to let the trim take the spotlight.

Pearl and beading foot

- Has a guide to feed round trims such as pearl and beads
- Use with all weights of fabric
- Match the needle size and type to the fabric and thread
- Use all-purpose, novelty, or invisible thread

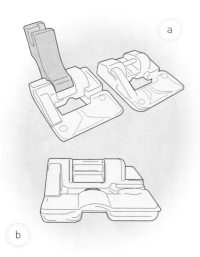

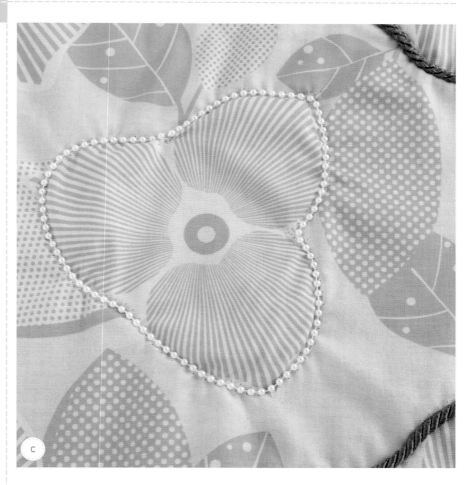

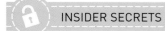

INSIDER SECRETS

You can also use a beading foot to feed piping and cording. It is great for stitching on rounded braided trims, for example, gimp braid.

The pearl and beading foot is a clear plastic foot with a round channel on the bottom to feed round trims such as strands of pearls and beads. It is available with different sizes of grooves such as ⅛" (3 mm) **(b)** and ¹⁄₁₆" (1.6 mm) **(a: screw-on left; snap-on right)** and you should use the appropriate size for the trim. This foot has a wide needle slot and you should use a zigzag stitch so that the needle stitches over the trim. You can use many types of threads, such as silk or metallic threads, with a beading foot to add a decorative element. Invisible thread is a good choice if you would like the trims to stand out **(c)**.

Binding foot

- Stitches binding around a fabric edge
- Can be used with single or double-fold tape
- Use with a universal 80/12 needle
- Use all-purpose polyester or cotton thread

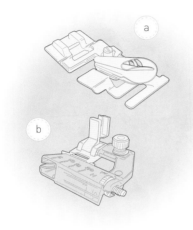

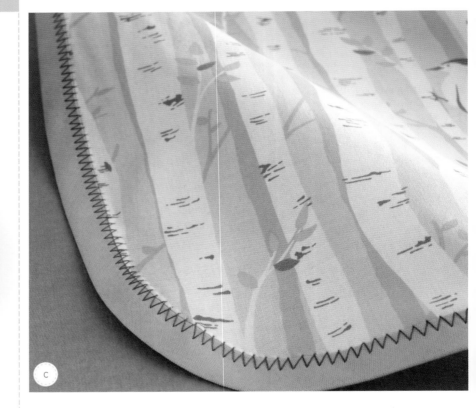

You can use a bias binder with basic straight stitches or you can be creative and use zigzag or decorative stitches. Make sure that your binder has a wide slot to accommodate stitches with width **(c)**.

The binding foot is also called a bias binder and is used for stitching double-fold and single-fold bias tape around a fabric edge. It eliminates the multistep process of stitching on the first edge of the tape and then wrapping the tape around to the back and stitching through the layers. Instead, the binding foot has a scroll through which you feed the tape and a center slot to feed the fabric edge. This foot can accommodate various widths of tape ranging from ¼" (6 mm) to ½" (1.3 cm) double-fold tape and 1" (2.5 cm) single-fold tape.

The traditional metal foot has a conical scroll with slots on the right **(a)**. Each slot is designated for a different size of double-fold tape, with the one closest to the needle for ¼" (6 mm). Working toward the needle, the slots are for ⁵⁄₁₆" (8 mm), ³⁄₈" (1 cm), ⁷⁄₁₆" (1.1 cm) and ½" (1.3 cm). The extra-large slot at the very end is for single-fold tape and it will fold the edges under. This foot also has a screw to adjust the position of the scroll to place the stitching near or far from the fold. You can also buy a clear plastic bias binder that works with wider tapes. It has a screw that adjusts the binding slot from narrow to wide tapes and a second screw to position the screw in relation to the needle **(b)**.

Fringe foot

- Creates loopy stitches as fringe
- Used to create tailor tacks to mark sewing details
- Match the needle type and size to the thread
- Use all-purpose thread or a decorative thread

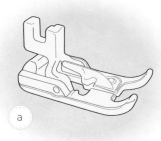

INSIDER SECRETS

Use a stitch that will clear the center blade, otherwise the needle will break. Always hand walk the needle by turning the hand wheel for a couple of stitches to double check.

The fringe foot looks like the stitch in the ditch foot because it has a fixed center blade between the toes. However, the blade of the fringe foot is tall and goes much closer to the needle (a). Zigzag stitches are formed over the blade, and when the fabric is removed from the machine, the stitches are loose loops (b). The loops can be left as a decorative stitch or they can be cut to form fringe. You can use the fringe foot to create pretty edges, stitch on appliqués, or emphasize seams. It is possible to adjust the width and length of the stitches to create different sizes and fullness of fringe and you can experiment with novelty threads such as variegated rayon or metallic threads.

The fringe foot is also useful for creating tailor tacks to mark sewing details such as darts or buttonhole placement. It is a good solution for fabrics that might be stained by a fabric marker or chalk. Use a silk thread so that the stitches can be easily removed when they are no longer needed.

Cording and couching

Couching is a beautiful embellishment technique in which you stitch down multiple strands of cord using a wide stitch. It is charming at a hem or cuff or it can be used as embroidery.

TOOLS

- Cording foot
- Needle threader
- Cording such as embroidery floss or fine yarn
- Invisible thread
- Fabric marker or tailor's chalk
- Tape measure
- Handsewing needle

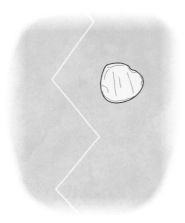

1 Draw a guideline on the fabric for the couching. It can be straight, curved, or in a shape.

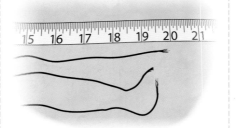

2 Cut a length of cord for each hole that you plan to use. Measure the design to determine the correct length and add a little extra.

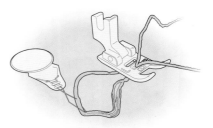

3 Thread the cord through the holes or guides on the cording foot. You may find it helpful to use a needle threader. If not using all the holes, then use the ones closest to the center.

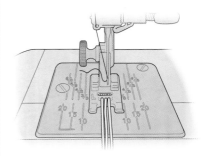

4 Install the cording foot and then thread the machine.

Trims and Embellishments

5 Select a three-step zigzag stitch with a stitch length of 2.5 mm.

6 With the lengths of cord out front, lower the presser foot onto the drawn line and start stitching.

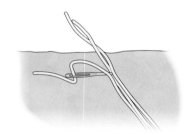

7 When you have finished, use the handsewing needle and threader to pull the cord and thread to the back side of the fabric and hand tie them off.

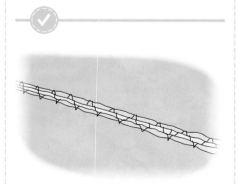

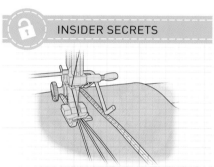

- If you are doing multiple rows of couching, use a quilting guide to keep the rows evenly spaced.

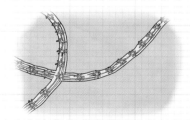

- Try using a decorative embroidery stitch in a contrasting color. Use variegated, metallic, or rayon embroidery thread for the upper thread and all-purpose thread in the bobbin. Make sure to use a needle appropriate to the thread.

Pintucks

Perfect pintucks are easy with a pintuck foot and make a lovely detail at hems, necklines, and sleeves or in home-décor projects such as pillows and curtains.

TOOLS

- Pintuck foot
- Two spools of all-purpose thread
- Twin needle
- Fabric marker or tailor's chalk
- Ruler
- Scissors or thread snips

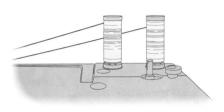

1 Install a twin needle and thread the machine with two spools of thread. You can also wind a second bobbin and use that as the second thread.

2 Install a pintuck foot and select a straight stitch with a stitch length of 2.5 mm.

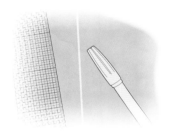

3 Mark the first row on the fabric using the marker or chalk and a ruler.

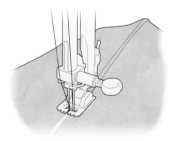

4 Stitch the first pintuck, making sure to backstitch at the beginning and end. Cut off the thread tails.

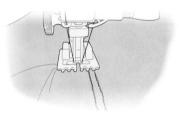

5 Insert the finished pintuck into one of the neighboring channels and stitch the next pintuck. Continue the process until all of the pintucks are complete.

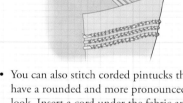

- You can also stitch corded pintucks that have a rounded and more pronounced look. Insert a cord under the fabric and then stitch pintucks as usual. Leave the cord in the pintuck.

- If you want pintucks on part of a garment, make sure to stitch the pintucks on the fabric and then cut out the garment piece to ensure the garment section is the correct size.

- Use a twin needle designed for the fabric. Use a stretch twin needle on knits and a universal twin needle on woven fabric. Widely spaced twin needles are better for heavier fabrics and closely spaced twin needles are suitable for lightweight fabrics.

Piping and welting

✿✿✿ Making piping and welting

Piping and welting are ideal ways to edge pillows but you can also use piping and welting as a design detail at necklines and armholes. You can insert them into a seam to emphasize seam lines.

TOOLS

- Piping or welting foot sized for the cording
- Cording
- Continuous bias strip
- All-purpose thread
- Pins

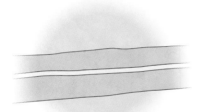

1 With the bias strip wrong side up, lay the cord in the middle.

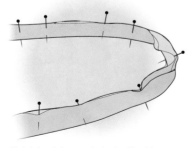

2 Fold the bias strip in half with wrong sides facing to encase the cord. Make sure the edges are lined up and pin to hold in place.

3 Thread the machine and put the piping or welting foot on the sewing machine.

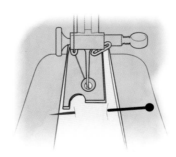

4 Select a basic straight stitch with a 2.5 mm length. Insert the cording into the groove and stitch, backstitching at the beginning and end. The stitch should be just to the right of the cord.

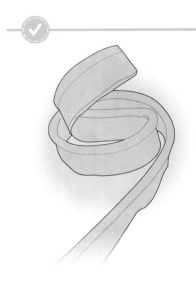

🔒 INSIDER SECRETS

If you don't have a piping foot, you can also use a zipper foot to make piping and welting. Place the zipper foot to the right of the cording and stitch very close to the cord.

Sewing on piping and welting

Piping and welting are ideal ways to edge pillows, but you can also use them as design details at necklines and armholes. You can insert them into a seam to emphasize seam lines.

TOOLS

- Piping or welting foot sized for the piping or welting
- Store-bought or handmade piping or welting
- All-purpose thread
- Pins
- Iron and ironing board

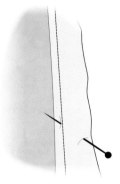

1 Lay the piping against the right side of the fabric piece to which it will be sewn. Make sure that the raw edges of the piping and the item are aligned and pin in place.

2 Put the piping or welting foot on the sewing machine.

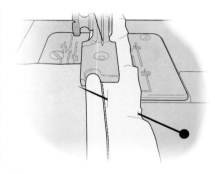

3 Line up the cording in the groove of the foot and lower the presser foot. Stitch along the edge of the cording.

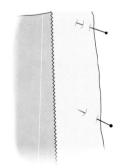

4 Place the lining or facing piece of fabric face down on top of the piping and pin it in place.

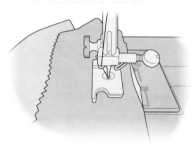

5 Again, line up the cording in the groove of the foot and lower the presser foot. Stitch through all the layers. Turn right side and press. Topstitch or edgestitch if desired.

Sewing on trims

 Ribbons, tapes, and sequin trims

Narrow flat trims such as ribbon, rickrack, and strands of sequins can all be machine topstitched onto fabric with a straight, zigzag, or decorative stitch.

TOOLS

- Tools
- Sequin and ribbon foot
- Fabric marker or tailor's chalk
- Ruler

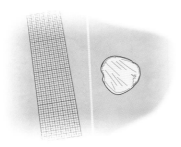

1 Mark placement for the trim onto the item on which it will be stitched using a ruler and chalk or marker.

2 Install the sequin and ribbon foot and thread the machine.

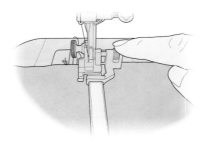

3 Insert the trim in the slot at the front of the foot and then adjust the position of the slot using the screw so that the trim is on the line and under the needle.

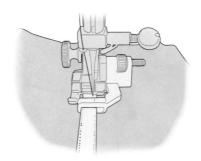

4 Select a straight, zigzag, or decorative stitch; lower the presser foot and stitch down the middle of the trim.

INSIDER SECRETS

You can also use a satin-stitch foot because the clear plastic allows for good visibility and the groove on the bottom allows space for trims. A satin-stitch foot may also be necessary if the trim is too wide for the guide on the sequin and ribbon foot.

Many wide ribbons look good when edgestitched, and you can do this easily and accurately using the blind hem foot.

TOOLS

- Blind hem foot
- Fabric marker or tailor's chalk
- Invisible, all-purpose, or novelty thread
- Ruler
- Pins

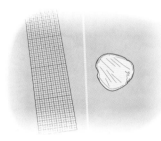

1 Using a ruler and chalk or marker, mark placement for the trim onto the fabric on which it will be stitched.

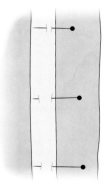

2 Pin the trim in place and select a straight, zigzag, or other stitch.

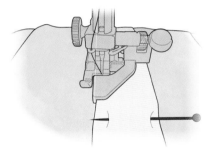

3 Put the blind hem foot on the machine. Using the hand screw, adjust the bar on the foot so that it comes right up against the left edge of the trim. With the needle in the center position, stitch the left edge of the trim.

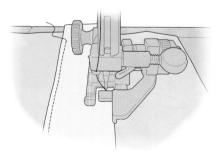

4 Adjust the bar on the blind hem foot until it comes to the right edge of the trim. Stitch down the right edge of the trim.

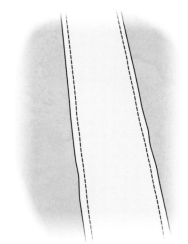

Using the pearl and beading foot

 ## Pearl and beaded trims

Strands of pearls and beads used to be tedious to sew because they had to be handsewed or glued onto fabric. A beading foot makes this task extremely simple and is perfect for bridal and special-occasion designs.

TOOLS

- Pearl and beading foot
- Fabric marker or tailor's chalk
- Ruler
- Invisible or matching all-purpose thread

1 Mark placement for the trim on the fabric using a ruler and chalk or marker.

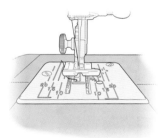

2 Install the pearl and beading foot and set the machine to a wide zigzag stitch with a length of 3 mm.

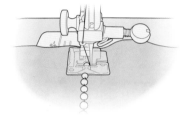

3 Lay the fabric under the foot with the guideline under the grove on the foot. Insert the bead in the groove and lower the foot.

4 Use the hand wheel to walk the machine a couple of stitches to ensure that the needle does not hit a bead, and adjust the stitch width as needed.

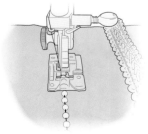

5 Stitch the trim in place, backstitching at the beginning and end.

 ### INSIDER SECRETS

Make sure to use an appropriately sized pearl and beading foot. The beads should slide easily through the groove, but not be too loose or they might move under the needle and break it.

 ## Yarn couching

The pearl and beading foot is also useful for couching down thick cords and yarns.

TOOLS

- Pearl and beading foot
- Fabric marker or tailor's chalk
- Ruler
- Invisible, matching, or contrasting thread

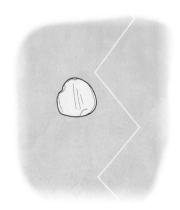

1 Mark placement for the trim on fabric using the ruler and chalk or marker.

2 Install the pearl and beading foot and set the machine to a wide zigzag stitch with a length of 3 mm.

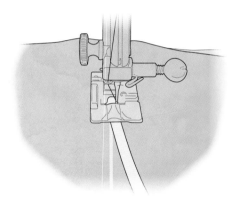

3 Lay the fabric under the foot with the guideline under the grove on the foot. Insert the cord or yarn in the groove, lower the foot, and adjust the stitch width as necessary.

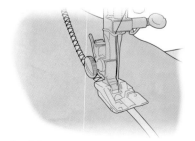

4 Stitch the trim in place, backstitching at the beginning and end.

INSIDER SECRETS

If you do not have a pearl and beaded foot, use a piping or satin-stitch foot.

Lace trims

There are many ways to stitch lace trims depending on the type of lace. Double-border lace trims can be topstitched onto fabric; single-border lace edgings can be inserted into a seam or used as an edging on hems, necklines, and sleeves.

TOOLS

- Sequin and ribbon foot
- Fabric marker or tailor's chalk
- Ruler
- Matching all-purpose thread or invisible thread

1 Using a ruler and chalk or marker, mark placement for the lace onto the item on which it will be stitched.

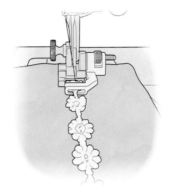

3 Insert the trim in the slot at the front of the foot and then adjust the position of the slot using the screw so that the trim is on the line and under the needle.

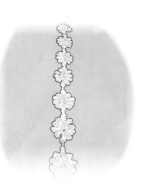

5 Select a straight, zigzag, or decorative stitch; lower the presser foot and stitch down the middle of the trim.

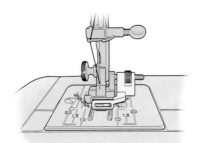

2 Install the sequin and ribbon foot and thread the machine.

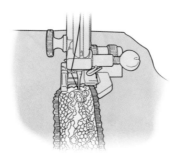

4 If the lace trim is too wide for the slot, slide it over the slot and under the foot.

Lace edgings are simply stitched onto the fabric edge with right sides facing and then flipped right side out and pressed. They can also be sandwiched between the fabric and a facing or lining.

How to make bias tape

Bias binding makes a neat and tidy finish to fabric edges. You can use it to hem a skirt or finish a neckline, or to bind bibs, blankets, and placemats. You can use purchased bias tape or you can easily make your own from any fabric.

TOOLS

- ½ yard (0.5 m) of 45" (114 cm) wide fabric to make approximately 9 yards (8 m) of ½" (1.3 cm)-wide double-fold bias tape
- Tailor's chalk or fabric marker
- Transparent ruler
- Pins
- Iron and ironing board
- Scissors or rotary cutter, cutting mat, and quilt ruler
- 1" (2.5 cm)-wide manual bias-tape maker

1 Fold over the selvedge to form a triangle, creating a 45-degree fold along the bias. Cut along that fold using either scissors or a rotary cutter, mat, and ruler.

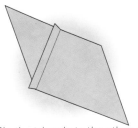

2 Pin the triangle to the other selvedge with right sides facing and stitch with a 1" (2.5 cm) seam allowance. Trim the seam allowances to ¼" (6 mm) and press open the seam allowances.

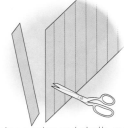

3 Using a ruler and chalk, mark parallel lines to the bias edge every 2" (5 cm) across the entire piece of fabric. Cut apart on the lines.

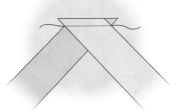

4 Take two strips of fabric and put the right sides of the fabric together. You need the tip of each strip to overhang by ¼" (6 mm); the two strips should make a 90-degree angle with each other.

5 Pin in place and stitch with a ¼" (6 mm) seam allowance. Repeat until all the pieces are stitched and you have one long piece. Press the seam allowances open.

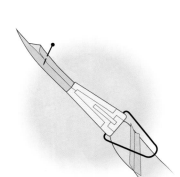

6 With the bias strip wrong side up, insert the strip into the wide end of the bias-tape maker.

7 Pull through to the small end, using a pin to help to guide it through. Pin the end to the ironing board to hold in place and keep both your hands free.

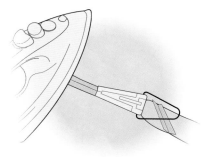

8 Start slowly pulling the bias-tape maker by the handle; the edges fold over toward the middle. Press the folds as you gently pull the bias-tape maker.

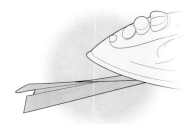

9 Press the finished strip again from the right side to set the folds. Now fold in half with wrong sides facing and one side a bit wider than the other. Press in place.

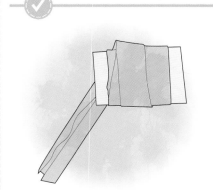

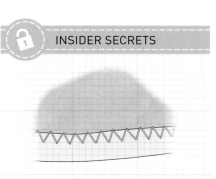

INSIDER SECRETS

Bias-tape makers come in many sizes ranging from ¼" (6 mm) to 2" (5 cm) wide. They only make single-fold bias tape, so keep in mind that double-fold tape will be half the width.

Bias binding

Applying prefolded bias tape

Using an all-purpose foot makes applying bias binding a multiple-step process of stitching, folding, ironing, pinning, and more stitching. You can apply bias binding in one simple step with a bias-binding foot.

TOOLS

- Bias-binding foot
- Purchased or handmade double-fold bias tape
- Matching all-purpose thread

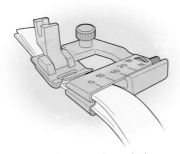

1 Feed the bias tape through the scroll on the bias-binding foot. You may need to use a pin to guide it through.

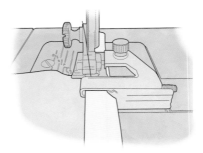

3 Insert the fabric edge into the main central slot and adjust the screw to position the bias tape so that the stitches are just to the right of the bias-tape fold.

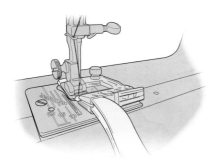

2 Install the bias-binding foot and select a straight stitch with a stitch length of 2.5 mm.

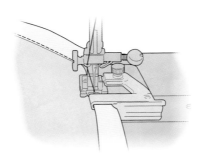

4 Lower the presser foot and start stitching, making sure to backstitch at the beginning and end.

INSIDER SECRETS

- You can also use a bias binder to attach foldover elastic to edges.

- You can choose decorative stitches to stitch down the bias tape. Try zigzag or embroidery stitches.

Trims and Embellishments

Applying unfolded bias tape

TOOLS

- Bias-binding foot with coil
- A flat, continuous bias strip
- Matching all-purpose thread

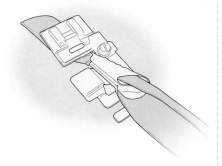

1 Feed the bias tape through the largest scroll on the end of bias-binding foot and install the foot.

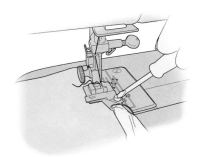

2 Insert the fabric edge into the main central slot and adjust the screw to position the bias tape so that the stitches are just to the right of the bias-tape fold.

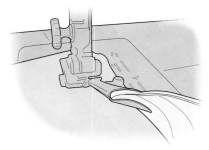

3 Lower the presser foot and start stitching, making sure to backstitch at the beginning and end.

 ### INSIDER SECRETS

This is an ideal way to bind seam allowances.

Fringe and tailor tacks

Fringe

The fringe foot creates loose and loopy stitches that can be used as a decorative stitch, appliqué stitch, and to create fringe. You can use all-purpose, topstitch, metallic, or embroidery thread.

TOOLS

- Fringe foot
- All-purpose foot
- Fabric marker or tailor's chalk
- Scissors
- Seam ripper

1 Thread the machine and loosen the upper tension to between 0 and 1.

2 Install the fringe foot and select a wide zigzag with a stitch length of 0.5 mm.

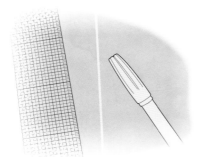

3 Use the marker or chalk to draw a guideline or design on the fabric.

4 Lower the presser foot and start stitching, making sure to backstitch at the beginning and end.

5 For fringe, switch to the all-purpose foot, set to a 2.5 mm-length straight stitch and adjust the tension to 4. Stitch down one side of the loops to secure.

6 On the wrong side, cut through the loops on the side with the straight stitch.

7 On the right side, use the seam ripper to gently loosen the fringe and fluff it up.

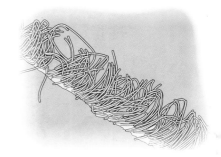

✿✿✿ Tailor tacks

Tailor tacks are used as pattern markings for dart points, pocket positioning, and button placement.

TOOLS

- Fringe foot
- Silk thread in a contrast color
- Scissors

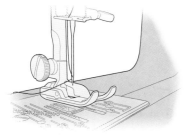

1 Install the fringe foot and thread the machine with the silk thread. Loosen the tension to 1.

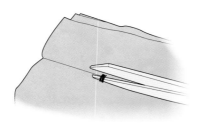

3 Carefully separate the two fabric layers and cut the threads between the layers to leave thread on each layer.

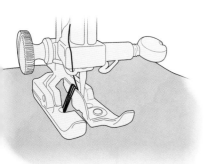

2 Select the widest zigzag stitch and a length of 0.5 mm. Stitch four to five stitches.

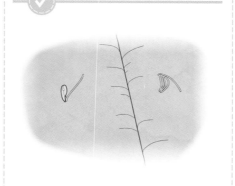

🔒 INSIDER SECRETS

Always carefully remove the fabric by pulling it from the back to slide the stitches off the blade.

Index

Acknowledgments

It was a pleasure to work with the team at RotoVision on this book. Thank you to Cath Senker and Jane Roe for editing all the text and making sure that all my explanations and tutorials made sense. Thank you to Emily Portnoi for art directing the book and making it so pretty. Extra special thanks to Sherry Heck for her beautiful photographs and for teaching me so much about photography and lighting. And lastly, thank you to Isheeta Mustafi for first approaching me to write this book. It has always been a dream of mine to do a project like this. I appreciate her patience as I learned the ropes of book publishing.

Thank you so much to all of the people who have taken a sewing class with me over the years. I have learned so much from my students because their questions force me to think of new ways to explain things. While writing this book I have shown my students all the different fancy feet and seen how excited they become as they master new skills. This has been a wonderful experience.

Thanks to my family and friends for understanding as I disappeared for weeks while doing research. Thank you especially to Vince for being so patient and supportive and always listening as I geeked out over my latest new sewing toy. And finally, thank you to my wonderful mom for buying me my first sewing machine when I was in fourth grade and for always telling me that I could do anything I set my heart and head to. This book is dedicated to you.